Galatians:
In Defense of Love
A Study Guide

Galatians:
In Defense of Love
A Study Guide

Mark J. Olson

Smyth & Helwys Publishing, Inc.

ISBN 1-880837-86-2

Copyright © 1994
Smyth & Helwys Publishing, Inc.

All rights reserved.
Printed in the United States of America.

Biblical quotations, unless otherwise noted, are from the New Revised Standard Version of the Bible, copyright © 1989 by the Division of Christian Education of the National Council of Churches of Christ in the U.S.A., and are used by permission.

The paper used in this publication
exceeds the minimum requirements of
American National Standard for Information Sciences-
Permanence of Paper for Printed Library Materials,
ANSI Z39.48-1984

Library of Congress Cataloging-in-Publication Data

Olson, Mark Jeffrey.
   Introducing Galatians: in defense of love. a study guide / Mark Olson. viii + 94 pp.   5.5 x 8.5"
   Includes bibliographical references.
   ISBN 1-880837-86-2
    1. Bible. N.T. Galatians—Study and teaching. I. Title.
BS26685.5.047 1994
227'.4407—dc20   94-10889
                                                        CIP

Contents

Preface		vii
Introduction		1
Chapter 1	Greeting and Attack! Galatians 1:1-10	13
Chapter 2	Paul's Autobiography: A Brief Sketch Galatians 1:11-2:10	23
Chapter 3	Justification by Faith Galatians 2:11-21	35
Chapter 4	Before Moses Came Abraham Galatians 3:1-18	45
Chapter 5	Why Give the Law If You Don't Want Legalism? Galatians 3:19-4:11	57
Chapter 6	Set Free by Christ Galatians 4:8-5:12	69
Chapter 7	Freedom Guided by Love Galatians 5:13-6:18	83

To Neal T. Jones, Pastor

and

Charles H. Talbert, Christian Scholar

Thank you for showing me a faith in Christ
that always seeks understanding

Preface

Galatians is a fiery letter—perhaps the most emotional letter that Paul ever wrote. I have tried to explain it without allowing my commentary to become a wet blanket that destroys that fire. Some of Paul's words may offend you, or inspire you, or even make you angry—and my job is not to tone down what he wrote. Instead, I hope that this commentary helps explain the vast differences between first-century Galatia and twentieth-century America so that the meaning and emotion of Paul's original words come through loud and clear! Once we understand the situation Paul faced, we can understand why his words sounded so desperate. Perhaps then we can begin asking how God can speak through these same words to a different people in a new day.

My wife Linda deserves much of the credit for any positive contribution that this book makes. She has shouldered far more than her share of the parenting duties these past months to allow me time to complete the manuscript. Our daughters, Kristin and Jaclyn, have been as understanding as little girls can be about daddy's absences. Dr. Harry Gamble first stimulated my interest in this crucial book during his 1985 Galatians seminar at the University of Virginia. More recently, many members of my congregation (First Baptist Church of South Boston, Virginia), as well as other friends, have guided me by reading Galatians and telling me what questions the letter raised for them. My secretaries, Alice Satterfield and Sylvia Knight, have corrected many of my mistakes, and my editor at Smyth and Helwys, Scott Nash, has been supportive and helpful throughout the process of publication.

Using This Book

I have written this commentary with the assumption that you will read the appropriate passage in Galatians first, then my words will make more sense. I have based my comments on the New Revised Standard Version (NRSV), but occasionally have referred to the New International Version (NIV) or offered my own translation from the Greek text. In each chapter you will find an introduction, verse-by-verse comments, a theological reflection, and questions for discussion.

Mark J. Olson
February 1994
South Boston, Virginia

Introduction

In an age that has largely forgotten how to write letters, it is amazing to discover a letter that has actually had a great impact for nearly 2000 years. Although we call it one of the sixty-six "books" of the Bible, Galatians was composed as a personal letter from Paul to Christians living in Galatia. They had been converted from paganism to faith in Christ when Paul had stopped in their area during one of his missionary journeys. Under his leadership they had formed a small church. After Paul had left, Christian missionaries with a different version of the faith came to Galatia. Paul heard about the newcomers and their proposed changes and blew up! For unknown reasons, he was unable to return to Galatia at that moment so he did the next best thing—he sent a letter. What a letter!

The Crucial Battle

Paul wrote his letter as a verbal blitzkrieg, an attack intended to overwhelm and destroy his opponents' position. He hoped the letter would persuade the Galatians to reject the viewpoint of his opponents and return to the version of Christianity that Paul had first preached to them.

The battle between Paul and his opponents was really a contest over one issue. Today we generally disparage "single-issue politics," but Paul believed that this one issue was crucial to the very existence of Christianity. It was a debate over the nature of salvation: "How can a person be saved?"

Paul had preached and then repeated in his letter the thesis that a person is saved by faith in Jesus Christ. We take that doctrine for granted so much today that it seems hard to believe that any other viewpoint was contemplated in the early church. Was it not it obvious to everybody that people were saved by faith in Christ alone? The answer is negative.

Historical Situation and Background

During the first two decades after Jesus' crucifixion and resurrection, most of the people who came to believe in Jesus as the messiah, or Christ, were Jews. Since Jesus was born Jewish, spent almost all of his time in Jewish territory, and addressed his preaching first to the Jews, it is not surprising that most of his early followers were Jews. Those followers included members of Jesus' band of twelve disciples such as Peter and John, family members such as Jesus' brother James, and many other men and women who decided that God had finally sent the long-awaited messiah. They did believe in Christ, and within a few years they were called "Christians" in his honor (Acts 11:26). Not one of these early followers would have said, "I am no longer a Jew." They were Jews who had found the Messiah that God had promised in the writings of the prophets. (For clarity we can refer to these followers as *Jewish Christians*. They can best be understood in comparison with the other Jewish sects that already existed.)

First-century Judaism was hardly a monolithic religion. It included various subgroups almost as varied as Protestant denominations in the twentieth century. The *Sadducees* emphasized temple worship and considered only the five books of Moses as scripture. They denied doctrines such as the resurrection, which could only be substantiated from the books of the prophets. Their emphasis upon temple worship led them to collaborate with the Romans to a greater degree than any other Jewish group. In effect, they gave support to the Roman Empire in return for assurances that the temple rituals would be allowed to continue unhindered.

The *Zealots* were quite different from the Sadducees. These men hated the Romans and saw Judaism's greatest goal as the liberation of the Promised Land from the pagans. They launched several minor revolts in the early part of the first century, but their greatest effort came nearly twenty years after Paul wrote Galatians. In A.D. 66, the Zealots led the Jewish nation into a suicidal war against the Roman Empire. After a few years, the Romans brought all of their might to bear against the Zealot-led Jewish forces, and in A.D. 70 they captured Jerusalem and destroyed the Temple.

The *Essenes*, one colony of which lived at Qumran near the Dead Sea, believed that all the other Jews had been corrupted by the Greco-Roman culture so they withdrew from society and built isolated colonies. This sect of Jews likely produced the famous Dead Sea Scrolls.

Most well-known were the *Pharisees*, Jewish laymen (not priests) who strove to apply the scriptural laws to daily life. Paul was one of the strictest members of this group. Because of their "negative press" in the gospels, they are universally scorned among Christians. At their best, however, these people tried to develop a version of Judaism that honored God in both religious ritual and ethical living. Despite their conflicts with Jesus, they were more like Jesus than any of the other groups.

Many Jews, especially among the *Palestinian peasants*, belonged to no one particular sect. They believed in God, worshiped at the synagogue, and hoped for the messiah. They did not know the scriptures like the Pharisees. They disliked Rome but found some Romans helpful. Most of all, they feared Rome's power so were not yet ready to risk their lives in a revolution. Frequently they traveled to Jerusalem for the major Jewish festivals such as Passover.

Against this background of various Jewish sects, one can easily see why *Jewish Christians* would be perceived as simply one more distinctive subgroup within Judaism. They were simply Jews who believed that a particular prophet from Galilee had been God's messiah. It was not obvious that a new world religion was emerging. As long as Jewish Christians maintained most of the distinctive traditions common to nearly all Jewish groups, their religion could conceivably remain a sect within Judaism for decades, if not centuries. Among these traditions were circumcision, food laws, Sabbath observance, and respect for scripture—especially the law of Moses. These traditions kept the Jewish people separate from the "Gentiles," a Jewish term for "everyone else."

When some Jewish Christians began to spread their faith in Jesus Christ to the Gentiles, however, the fault line opened wide. Gentiles could not be admitted to any Jewish sect unless they converted to Judaism, and this involved circumcision and obedience to food laws at a minimum. If Gentile "converts" did not acknowledge these, then the distinctiveness of Judaism would be lost.

Paul did not see Jewish Christianity as one Jewish sect among many but as *the one true sect* within Judaism. Furthermore, he saw faith in Christ as being so overwhelmingly important that the other "distinctives" of Judaism faded into comparative insignificance. It was far more important that Gentiles be won to faith in Christ than to maintain the other distinctives of Judaism. For this truth Paul was willing to fight. He launched a frontal assault against his opponents, the *Judaizers*, who probably thought they were simply trying to make sure the church in Galatia became loyal to Judaism as well as to the Jewish messiah.

Who Were Paul's Opponents?

Exactly who were these opponents, the *Judaizers*? They were Jewish Christians who tried to make Gentiles follow at least a few basic requirements of the law of Moses. They believed that Jesus was the messiah but wanted all Christians to remain under the larger umbrella of Judaism. Apparently they did not demand that the Gentile Christians in Galatia follow every one of the laws of Moses found in scripture. Instead, they emphasized a few regulations they deemed especially important. Foremost among these was circumcision, but food laws and Sabbath observances were probably stressed as well.

Some scholars have hypothesized that Paul was arguing against two distinct groups of opponents: Judaizers and *Gnostics*. Gnostics (pronounced "Nostics") were Christian heretics of the second, third, and fourth centuries who combined elements of Christianity with a bit of Greek philosophy and a large dose of mystical imagination. They produced bizarre "gospels" and other writings that stressed that all matter was evil and, therefore, that Christ was a redeemer without a physical body or physical resurrection. Since the God of the Old Testament created the "evil" physical world, many Gnostics concluded that God was an evil God who was in competition with the good God who sent Christ. Having discarded monotheism, many Gnostics imagined dozens of gods, typically in pairs.

As you read Galatians, see if you discover hints that Paul was fighting against Gnostics as well as Judaizers. I find no such evidence. Although the Greek word translated "elemental spirits" in Galatians 4:9 was used later by Gnostics to refer to some of the minor gods or demons they created in their imaginative writings, Paul was probably using the phrase to refer to "elemental principles" of the Judaizers. We have no substantial evidence that any true Gnostics were numbered among Paul's opponents. The book of Galatians makes better sense if explained as a letter in which Paul attacked one particular group of opponents—the Judaizers.

Where and When Was Galatians Written?

We do not know where Galatians was written. Apparently Paul was not in prison, as he was when he wrote several other letters, but that is all we can say.

Questions of date are rather complex and intertwined with the larger questions of the chronology of Paul's entire life. If this commentary has correctly interpreted the first two chapters of Galatians, then the letter was written shortly after Paul left his new cluster of churches in southern Galatia, which he founded on his first missionary journey (Acts 13:14-14:23). This would place the date approximately A.D. 49. Other scholars argue that Paul wrote the letter to churches in northern Galatia, which he founded on his second or third missionary journey. Most of these scholars date Galatians about A.D. 54. This difference of about five years is more important to the scholars than to you. Either way, amazingly, a letter written for one small group of people 1900 years ago now speaks powerfully to millions of people in the twentieth century.

The Continuing Significance of Galatians

Throughout Christian history, Galatians has been more influential than its short length would suggest. Many of the great biblical interpreters of the ancient, medieval, and Reformation periods wrote commentaries upon it. Luther considered it one of the chief epistles of the New Testament because of its emphasis on justification by faith. How can we evaluate Galatians today?

Along with Romans, Galatians stands as the great barrier to anyone who hopes to turn Christianity into a legalistic system. Paul's fiery warnings against the legalism of the Judaizers have been used against more modern types of legalism as well.

In the sixteenth century, the Catholic monk Tetzel tried to turn salvation into something that could be earned or purchased through the sale of papal indulgences. He found

Luther using Galatians to attack his perversion of the gospel.

In our time, some fundamentalists (not all) would like to turn Christianity into a rigid set of rules and regulations. Paul's emphasis on freedom over law will always cause these people difficulty. Galatians simply cannot be reconciled with any legalistic system. On the other hand, many church members today would like to indulge in our society's libertine "freedoms." This self-centered pursuit of every sensual pleasure was certainly not what Paul meant by "freedom." These people need to read Paul's contrasting descriptions of the "works of the flesh" and the "fruit of the Spirit" in Galatians 5:16-26.

Galatians does not give a balanced portrait of Paul. Philemon shows the more sensitive side of the apostle. First Corinthians shows that he opposed hedonism as staunchly as he did legalism. Romans relates justification by faith more fully to the rest of Paul's theology. We need to read all of these letters to take the full measure of the man, but Galatians still gives the heart of his theology. Galatians still shows the decisive battle that guaranteed the vast majority of the world's population access to salvation in Jesus Christ.

Rome
Italy
Puteoli
Paestum
Croton
Sicily
Syracuse
Malta
Macedonia
Philippi
Thessalonica
Neapolis
Apollonia
Troas
Beroea
Athens
Sparta
Smyrna
Assos
Ephesus
Miletus
Cos
Sindus
Patara
Crete
Black Sea
Galatia
Dorylaeum
Cappadocia
Antioch
Iconium
Perga
Derbe
Attala
Myra
Antioch
Syria
Salamis
Paphos
Damascus
Caesarea
Jerusalem
Mediterranean Sea
Nabataeans

A Brief Chronology*
Relating to Galatians

Crucifixion and resurrection of Jesus Christ	30
Paul's conversion	33
First Jerusalem visit	36
Second Jerusalem visit	47
Paul and Barnabas establish churches in Galatia	48
Judaizers arrive in Galatia	48–49
Paul writes Galatians	49
Jerusalem Conference regarding the Gentile Christians	49

*(all dates are approximate A.D.)

For Further Reading

Betz, Hans Dieter. *Galatians: A Commentary on Paul's Letter to the Churches in Galatia*. Philadelphia: Fortress, 1979. Betz's massive commentary focuses much attention on an analysis of Paul's letter as an example of Greek rhetoric. It is more helpful in understanding the organization of the letter than it is in explaining the essence of Paul's argument.

Bruce, F. F. *The Epistle to the Galatians*. New International Greek Testament Commentary. Grand Rapids MI: Eerdmans, 1982. This volume is thoroughly researched and well-written, as one expects of Bruce. The format is not as easy to use as the Word Biblical Commentary.

Cousar, Charles. *Galatians*. Interpretation. Louisville KY: John Knox, 1982. A bit lighter than Longenecker or Betz, Cousar writes clearly and is especially good at dealing with the larger thought-units of the letter. Sometimes it is difficult to find his comments about a particular verse without reading an entire section of his commentary.

Longenecker, Richard N.. *Galatians*. Word Biblical Commentary. Dallas: Word, 1990. This is the best commentary on Galatians available. Although written on the Greek text, English translations are always given. The concluding "explanation" sections will prove particularly helpful to laypeople.

Sanders, E. P. *Paul and Palestinian Judaism: A Comparison of Patterns of Religion*. Philadelphia: Fortress, 1977. Not for the faint-hearted, this work changed the way most scholars understand first-century Judaism. Sanders shows that most ancient Jews did not think they had earned their own salvation, but rather many obeyed the law as a dedicated response to God's gracious giving of the covenant.

Westerholm, Steven. *Israel's Law and the Church's Faith: Paul and His Recent Interpreters*. Grand Rapids MI: Eerdmans, 1988. Galatians is all about Paul and "the law," which has been a major issue of scholarly debate for the past decade. Westerholm surveys the various scholarly positions in a clear and concise manner before giving his own particular reading of Paul's view of the law. It is excellent!

Chapter 1

Greeting and Attack!

Galatians 1:1–10

Although the juxtaposition of the two words, "greeting" and "attack," may seem strange, you will understand the relationship after reading the first ten verses of Galatians. The book begins with a typical greeting but very quickly jumps to Paul's real purpose in writing—attacking those who were preaching a gospel different from the one he preached when he founded the Galatian churches. A few key questions are posed: What exactly was the false teaching that made Paul angry enough to curse? Who were the people responsible for teaching this different gospel? Was the argument really over a "different gospel," or was Paul simply overreacting because the Galatian Christians were following the leadership of someone else? The answers to these questions may not come until we have read nearly all of Galatians, but our study will be more profitable if we keep these key questions in mind while we read this first section of Paul's letter.

Comment

1   For twentieth-century Americans, finding the author's name at the beginning of a letter seems strange because we sign our names at the end of the letter. If you

have ever received a long letter from someone whose name did not appear on the outer envelope, however, you probably turned immediately to the last page to see who the writer was. Paul and other ancient writers eliminated that problem by putting the author's name at the beginning.

We have grown so accustomed to thinking of Paul as an apostle that we read right over the opening words, "Paul, an apostle," without giving them a second thought. Some early Christians challenged Paul's status as one of *the* apostles, however. After all, he was not one of the original twelve disciples, nor was he chosen to replace Judas after that disciple's tragic suicide. After Christ's resurrection, the disciples were often referred to as "the twelve apostles," and Paul was clearly not one of them. Paul was not even one of the many Jews who had followed Jesus around Galilee to hear him preach and see him perform miracles. On what basis could he claim the lofty title of "apostle"? Would Peter and John have granted him the right to the same title held by themselves and the rest of "the twelve"?

Paul answered that challenge in detail later in an autobiographical section (1:11-2:14), but in verse 1 he gave the readers a hint of what will come. The Greek word, *apostolos*, which we simply transliterate into English as "apostle," means "one who is sent," or "messenger." Paul based his claim to be an apostle on the fact that God had sent him out with a message. His commissioning as an apostle did not come from Peter, John, or any other human authority, but came "through Jesus Christ and God the Father." How that commissioning came, Paul did not explain, except that he briefly referred to Christ's resurrection. Later he explained the connection between Christ's resurrection and his own commissioning as an apostle.

2 Paul often mentioned other Christians who were with him as he wrote (see 1 Cor 1:1 and Phil 1:1). Unfortunately for us, none are named here. If he had included their names, that data might have helped us pinpoint Paul's location when he wrote this letter. We know that one person with Paul was his secretary or scribe, who wrote the entire letter for Paul until 6:11 when Paul took the pen in his own hand; but neither the scribe nor the other Christians with Paul are mentioned by name.

The question of exactly which churches of Galatia Paul addressed has been discussed at length in the introduction. Most likely he was writing to the churches at Iconium, Lystra, Derbe, and Antioch of Pisidia—churches of southern Galatia that Paul founded on his first missionary journey, as recorded in Acts, and visited on his second journey. (Your study will be helped considerably if you examine the map on page 9 and read the corresponding travel narratives in Acts 13:14-14:23 and 16:1-6).

This conclusion cannot be certain, and many scholars maintain that Paul's letter was really directed to churches in northern Galatia. Possibly, references to Galatia in Acts 16:6 and 18:23 might mean that Paul also founded churches in some of the cities of northern Galatia (near Ankara, the capital of modern Turkey). The debate between northern and southern Galatia, ironically, is more an argument about chronology than about geography. Scholars who believe that Paul wrote to the churches of southern Galatia usually suggest that Paul wrote Galatians shortly after he founded the southern churches on his first missionary journey. If this is true, Galatians was written in the late forties A.D., making it Paul's oldest surviving letter. Scholars who defend the northern Galatia hypothesis usually suggest that

Paul wrote it late in his third missionary journey—during the mid-fifties.

3   Some variant of the phrase, "grace to you and peace from God our Father," is found in every letter that Paul wrote, including Galatians. (Even the letters of disputed Pauline authorship, like the Pastorals, have a form of the same phrase.) "Grace" was probably used because it communicated Paul's basic understanding of salvation and closely resembled another Greek term for "greetings." "Peace," although written in Greek, surely reflects Paul's Jewish background where the Hebrew greeting *shalom* was commonly used.

4–5   Later in the letter we will hear so much about "justification" that it may appear Paul only used legal metaphors to describe salvation, but in verses 4 and 5 he painted a picture of Christ rescuing us from the "present evil age." Today we think of freedom as the right to make our own choices in a world full of good and evil options; Paul thought otherwise. He saw the world as dominated by evil forces that overpowered people and held them captive. If he visited America today he would no doubt point to the cocaine addicts, the yuppies pursuing "financial security," and the Arnie Beckers (of T.V.'s *L.A. Law*) pursuing sexual fulfillment. These people, he would say, think they are free but are not. Their "freely made choices" have enslaved them. Fortunately, God's own will was to have Christ truly set us free by giving himself on the cross "for our sins."

6   At this point in most of his letters, Paul added a thanksgiving to his opening greeting (see Rom 1:8-15 and Phil 1:3-11). He had just finished praising God for Christ's willingness to die "for our sins," but he gave no praise to the Galatians themselves. Even when he needed to rebuke the Corinthian church for numerous sins and mistakes, he

first took time to commend them (1 Cor 1:4-9). In Galatians Paul totally ommitted his typical thanksgiving section, however, and plunged straight into a stern rebuke—hence the title, "Greeting and Attack!"

Obviously Paul had just received word, in person or by letter, of recent developments within the churches of Galatia. New Christian missionaries apparently had arrived with a different message from the one Paul preached to the Galatians. What was the content of their message? Only as we read further in the letter will we be able to reconstruct the teachings of those missionaries. For now we can simply conclude that Paul believed their message was very dangerous; it encouraged the Galatians to desert God's message of grace in Christ for "another gospel."

7 Paul quickly realized that his words in verse 6 could be easily misunderstood. Since the Greek term for "gospel," *euangelion,* means "good news," Paul was essentially saying that these rival missionaries brought a different type of "good news" with them. Paul thought their message was really *bad news,* so he immediately qualified his earlier statement. The only one true "good news" or "gospel" was the one Paul preached. The rival message simply confused confessing Christians and perverted the true faith.

8–9 In verses 8 and 9, Paul's anger burst beyond the bounds of civil discourse. He dogmatically pronounced a curse upon anyone, even an "angel from heaven," who preached a message contrary to Paul's gospel. So angry was the former Pharisee that he repeated the curse a second time! What are we to make of such angry language?

Today we hear that kind of rhetoric from pro-life and pro-choice demonstrators at an abortion clinic, and most of us are offended by the language of both sides. Politicians vehemently characterize their opponents with negative T.V.

ads, and we cringe. We certainly do not expect such language in church, yet here it is in the Bible—God's holy word! To turn Paul's favorite term against him, what justification could he offer for using such polemical language?

Two observations will have to suffice. First, the burden of proof is on Paul to show that his opponents' message was so dangerous as to warrant this angry rebuke. Second, Jesus himself angrily denounced the Pharisees, drove the money changers out of the temple with a whip, and even told his key disciple to "get behind me Satan!" Therefore, we can conclude that Jesus did approve of angry denunciations in some situations, especially when religious leaders were misleading God's people. Whether or not Paul's opponents were really dangerously misleading the people remains to be seen.

10 Verse 10 is nearly opaque at first reading, thus necessitating a second reading. What does this verse mean? It seems to break the flow of thought and serves as a very abrupt transition from the denunciation of Paul's opponents in the previous verses to the defense of his own calling in the verses that follow. Hearing this verse is like hearing half of a telephone conversation. Paul was defending himself against a charge.

What was the charge? Perhaps his opponents, those as yet unidentified missionaries, had accused Paul of being a people-pleaser. Maybe they accused him of perverting the gospel to make it easier for people to accept. In 1 Corinthians 10:33, Paul spoke in favor of trying to please others: "I try to please everyone in everything I do, not seeking my own advantage, but that of many, so that they may be saved," but here in Galatians he clearly stated that his first priority was not to please others but to please his master—God. Since slavery has been abolished in our time, modern translators usually translate the Greek term, *doulos*, as "servant." Surely the Galatian Christians would have read the term as "slave." How ironic that, in a letter known for its emphasis on freedom, Paul the Roman citizen boldly claimed the status of one who had no freedoms in Roman society—a slave, a slave of Christ!

Theological Reflection

The key issues in this opening section of Galatians are *authority* and *conflict*. By what authority did Paul preach the gospel? Who gave him the authority to write so dogmatically? His double curse in verses 8-9 raises the question of conflict management. Was Paul's poignant criticism of his rival missionaries the best way to deal with conflicting understandings of the gospel? When he heard that these new missionaries were altering aspects of his teaching, did Paul overreact and respond in anger unnecessarily?

Two modern examples may help illuminate the dilemma that Paul faced. The first comes from the schism within the Southern Baptist Convention. Fundamentalist Baptists determined that the authority of the Bible was being undermined by biblical scholars using the historical critical method. They then attacked everyone who had written or said anything that sounded like a challenge to the authority of scripture. One elder statesman of the fundamentalist movement called all the moderate Baptists "skunks!" His anger at the moderates erupted in heated rhetoric, just like Paul's anger erupted.

The second example is found in the pages of the "Letter From a Birmingham Jail" by Martin Luther King, Jr. He, too, erupted in anger at moderate Christians (Baptists and members of other denominations as well)—in this case for their refusal to actively support his efforts at racial integration. Because of their passivity, King suggested that the white moderates might be a greater stumbling block to the black Americans' "stride toward freedom" than the KKK.[1]

Two Christian leaders who claimed God's authority for their message. Two conflicts. Two stringent attacks upon their opponents. Is there any difference between the conflicts? Is there a lesson to be learned? The key issue is the truth or falsehood of each indictment. In the first case, many of the scholars, pastors, and laypeople who were labeled "skunks" were actually trying to uphold the authority of the Bible and demonstrate its relevance for today. The charge of undermining the authority of scripture, while perhaps true in a few cases, was not warranted as a blanket accusation of all moderate Baptists. In the second case, King's accusation was true for the great majority of moderates. They were too timid, too passive on the issue of racial integration. They were afraid of what their neighbors and friends would say or what the KKK might do, so they refused to take the bold stand. King's authority to "attack" came from the truth of his indictment.

What can we conclude about Paul? Did he have the authority to make these harsh indictments on rival Christian missionaries? Did he unjustly allow his angry rhetoric to spill onto those who held a different perspective, as in the first example cited above? Or was his indignation justified, as with King? The first ten verses of Galatians simply do not provide enough information to decide the question. The burden of proof was with Paul to convince his readers that the variant message of the rival Christian missionaries was dangerous and merited such caustic condemnation. Paul needed to convince us that he was speaking the truth and had God's own authority on his side. That task is discussed in 1:11-2:14.

Questions for Discussion

1. How do you define the term "apostle"? Do you use it to refer only to "the twelve" or also to other missionaries like Paul and Barnabas?

2. Is a Christian ever justified in displaying anger? If so, how serious would the situation in Galatia have had to be to justify Paul's angry words? If not, how do you explain Jesus' occasional displays of anger?

3. There are obviously many different Christian denominations: Catholic, Presbyterian, Methodist, Assemblies of God, Episcopal—to name a few. Would you also say there are different "gospels," or is there only one "gospel"?

4. Do you feel comfortable thinking of yourself as a "slave of Christ"? Why or why not?

Note

[1] Martin Luther King, Jr., *Why We Can't Wait* (New York: Mentor, 1963) 84.

Chapter 2

Paul's Autobiography: A Brief Sketch

Galatians 1:11–2:10

Following the angry intoduction, Paul changed his focus and began to give his life story in short form. Students of history love this section because it not only gives invaluable information about Paul but also provides historical data that can be compared with the information about the early church in the book of Acts. This passage is crucial for scholars attempting to reconstruct Pauline chronology, for those who want a glimpse of how conflict was handled in the early church, and for those who wonder if Galatians was the first-written of all of Paul's letters.

What about that majority of Americans who find historical details boring and dull? What about those who do not care if Galatians was written in A.D. 49 or 54? Is there anything in this section for those who care more for theology than history, who want first to ask the question of contemporary relevance: "How does this relate to my life today?" Should these people skip this passage? No!

This section, which seems filled with historical minutiae, gives the key to Paul's entire theology. Paul was no academic theologian, visiting libraries and composing learned volumes for other scholars of religion to read. He was an activist, a traveling preacher, a daring missionary to "unreached people-groups." His theology was intensely personal; he recorded it as it overflowed from his life experiences. In this autobiographical sketch, Paul revealed the key event that changed his life and altered almost every element of his theology.

Comment

11-12 Echoing the first lines of his letter, Paul insisted that his message was not of human origin. This point is crucial to his entire argument. If his message or gospel had been received from others, his opponents could have argued that Paul's authority was derivative, that he was subordinate to those who initially gave him the gospel message. Furthermore, if they could have demonstrated that Paul deviated from what he was told by others, then they could have accused him of perverting the gospel message. Paul defended against this line of attack by raising his defense to a higher level. He claimed that his message had come directly from Jesus Christ by means of a revelation.

13 Verse 13 begins to tell what Paul's life was like before he became a Christian. Consider the situation after Jesus' crucifixion and resurrection. One group of Jews, led by Peter and the other disciples, believed Jesus' claim to be the promised messiah. We may refer to the members of this first group as Jewish Christians.

A second group of Jews, probably the majority, took a basically neutral stance toward the Jewish Christian group. This group's viewpoint was articulated by the Pharisee Gamaliel in Acts 5:34-39: "Keep away from these men and let them alone; because if this plan or this undertaking is of human origin, it will fail; but if it is of God, you will not be able to overthrow them."

The third group was small but fanatical. Its members charged that Jesus' messianic claims were blasphemous, and they violently persecuted the Jewish Christians who believed in him. They threw some Jewish Christians in jail and, in the most extreme case, stoned Stephen to death. Acts tells us that Paul participated in the killing and was a leader of this group (7:58-60). (Note that these verses use the Jewish form of Paul's name, Saul.)

14 Why did Paul react so violently against the Jews who followed Jesus? The key is found in verse 14. Paul took the traditions of his Jewish ancestors—the written and oral Law—more seriously than his peers did. Elsewhere, Paul revealed that his parents obeyed the letter of the law and had him circumcised on the eighth day after he was born (Phil 3:5). They must have impressed upon him the importance of following the law scrupulously. When he grew up, Paul joined the Pharisees, a group of Jewish laymen who strove to live by God's law in daily life. According to his own testimony, Paul followed the law more scrupulously than any of the other Jews he knew. He learned it and lived it so well that he considered himself to be blameless before God—"as to righteousness under the law, blameless" (Phil 3:6).

Many biblical interpreters have assumed that Paul's conversion experience must have been similar to Martin Luther's conversion. Before he "discovered" God's grace, Luther was racked by guilt and fearful of damnation for the smallest sins. Since Luther experienced a tremendous release from guilt while reading Paul's letters, we can easily understand why some persons would assume that Paul must also have been racked by guilt before his conversion.

That is not what Paul said, however. The pre-conversion Paul and pre-conversion Luther had totally different attitudes. Luther tried to live a perfectly righteous life but was constantly aware of his failures. His one word for himself was "sinner!" Paul also strove to live a perfectly righteous life by following God's law as found in the scriptures and oral traditions of the rabbis. He believed himself to be successful. His one word for himself?—"Righteous!"

15-17 This self-evaluation changed radically when God revealed the Son to Paul. Apparently Paul had previously shared with the Galatians the details of his conversion experience with the resurrected Christ on the road to Damascus, so he did not need to repeat the story. Without the details of the account found in Acts 9:1-22, we would know nothing of the blinding light and Jesus' life-shattering question: "Saul, Saul, why do you persecute me?" This was the question that changed Paul's life and forced him to rethink all of his theology. This zealous Pharisee, who followed the law so intensely that he *knew* he stood righteous before God, discovered that he was God's antagonist! His thoroughgoing obedience to the law's smallest commands had led him into direct opposition to the Almighty. Never again did he view obedience to the letter of the law in the same way.

Note that Paul's conversion, though certainly personal, was not individualistic—that is, it did not involve only Paul and God. God's revelation of the risen Christ included the further revelation that Paul was to become a preacher to the Gentiles. This Pharisee, whose devotion to the law had kept him separated from unclean Gentiles, was commanded to go and preach to the very people he had despised. The closest modern parallel would be if God revealed the truth to the most bigoted white Christian in a particular church and not only changed that person's attitude about blacks, but sent him/her into the work of interracial ministry.

17-19 The Acts narrative gives an account of Paul's post-conversion activities that differs significantly from Paul's own version. The differences can best be seen in a side-by-side comparison:

Acts 9	Galatians
Paul's conversion	Paul's conversion Did not go to Jerusalem Went to Arabia
Preached in Damascus Fled Damascus Went to Jerusalem	Returned to Damascus Went to Jerusalem 3 years later
Met "apostles"	Met Cephas (Peter) and James

What conclusions can we draw from examining these two quite different itineraries? A strident claim that both narratives must be historically inerrant is simply not convincing. Paul's version should be preferred because it is a first-person account, whereas Luke reported events secondhand. Furthermore, Paul wrote his account within twenty years of his conversion, but Acts was probably not written until forty or fifty years after the Damascus Road experience. Luke either did not know about Paul's journey into Arabia and return to Damascus or else intentionally omitted these details because they seemed to be of secondary importance.

20 Obviously, someone did *not* prefer to believe Paul's account! Some of his opponents must have claimed that he lied to cover the fact that he received instruction and commissioning from the apostles in Jerusalem. Paul insisted that this was not so. He had already been a Christian for three years when he met Peter and James in Jerusalem, and even then he only stayed for fifteen days.

21-24 Next Paul preached in Syria and then in his home province of Cilicia, of which Tarsus was the capital (see the map on page 9). Unfortunately, he gave no details of his homecoming in Cilicia because his intent was not to retell the story of his missionary journeys. Rather, Paul wanted to prove that he had always been independent of the Jerusalem apostles. He insisted that even in those early years of ministry to the Gentiles, the Judean churches around Jerusalem heard gladly of his evangelistic successes.

It is hard to believe that most of the Christians in the Jerusalem area did not know what Paul looked like. Yet, in the days before television, newspaper photos, and *People* magazine, it was common to know the names of notable people, and even details of their accomplishments, without having any idea of their appearance.

2:1 Did Paul mean that his second Jerusalem visit occurred fourteen years after his conversion (1:15) or fourteen years after his first visit there (1:18)? Since either meaning is grammatically possible in Greek, we simply do not know. All we can conclude with certainty is that this second Jerusalem visit must have occurred in the mid-forties A.D. (Readers interested in historical details may wish to study the chronological chart on page 10. Remember that any such reconstruction contains a good bit of scholarly guesswork; the dates are nearly all speculative, even if they appear in the pages of a study Bible.)

The key point, again, is that before this crucial meeting took place in Jerusalem Paul had already been preaching for fourteen or seventeen years. He expected the Galatian readers to note that his account of the events in Jerusalem could be backed up by two witnesses who were there with him, Barnabas and Titus.

2 What does Acts tell us about this visit to Jerusalem, which Galatians indicates was Paul's second such trip? That depends on whether you decide that the events Paul described occurred during the visit alluded to in Acts 11:27-30 or the one detailed in Acts 15:2-23. Scholars are about evenly divided in their decisions. Because Galatians 2 and Acts 15 both describe debates between Paul and some of the apostles concerning the Gentile mission, many scholars have concluded that these two passages describe the same visit to Jerusalem. They discount the Acts 11 visit by assuming either that Paul forgot to mention that particular visit in Galatians, or that Luke confused Paul's itinerary and recounted a later visit in Acts 11.

The more likely scenario is that Acts 11 and Galatians 2 both describe Paul's second visit to Jerusalem, and Acts 15 describes his third visit to the city. If this guess is correct, then the "revelation" in verse 2 was that received by the Christian prophet Agabus (see Acts 11:27-28). In response to Agabus' prediction of a famine, Paul and Barnabas were sent to Jerusalem with aid from the church at Antioch. While in Jerusalem, Paul met privately with key leaders of the Jerusalem church to explain the gospel message he was proclaiming to the Gentiles.

3 Even though the Jerusalem church was composed of Jewish Christians who still practiced circumcision, the members did not insist on circumcising Titus, Paul's Gentile Christian assistant. (In this verse "Greek" means

"Gentile".) By accepting an uncircumcised believer as a Christian, argued Paul, the Jerusalem leaders were implicitly admitting that circumcision was not necessary for salvation in Christ.

4-5 Just remembering that certain "false brothers" tried to sneak in and oppose his mission to the Gentiles made Paul sputter with anger. His sentence is grammatically confused but accurately conveys the intense emotion Paul felt during the argument.

6 Paul's opponents were unnamed Judaizers, but the key decision-makers in the Jerusalem church were the Lord's brother James,[1] Peter (called by his Aramaic name Cephas), and John.

7-9 These three key apostles, who had led the Jerusalem church in its efforts to convert Jews to faith in Christ, accepted Paul and Barnabas as missionaries to the Gentiles. This acceptance at least tacitly included an acknowledgement that any Gentiles who accepted Christ would not have to obey the Jewish law—that is, they would not have to be circumcised or observe Jewish food regulations. Furthermore, Paul emphasized that this was no half-hearted, reluctant concession by James, Peter, and John. All three indicated full acceptance of the Gentile mission by giving Paul and Barnabas "the right hand of fellowship."

10 Their request that Paul remember the poor was fully honored by the man from Tarsus. Later in his ministry, Paul spent several years collecting another famine relief offering for the Jerusalem church from the very Gentile Christian churches he founded (1 Cor 16:1-3; 2 Cor 8:1-15; Rom 15:25-29). In fact, Paul saw that second offering as an opportunity to complete the circle: the blessings God had brought to the Gentiles through the Jews and the Jewish messiah would return to the Jews through the generous financial offering the Gentile churches sent to Jerusalem.

Theological Reflection

Although the term "resurrection" never appears in this section of Galatians, Paul's experience with the resurrected Christ permeates every verse. The Galatians knew the details of that experience through the sermons Paul had previously preached in Galatia. We know some of the story via the account in Acts 9, but the key is to look beneath the historical event, as important as that was (and is!), and consider how profoundly Paul was changed by his experience with the resurrected Christ.

The Pharisee who once rigorously observed all the laws now preached freedom from the law. The one who hated "unclean" Gentiles now reached out to them and ate meals with them. The zealous persecutor of the church now proclaimed the faith he had tried to destroy. In Paul's story we find the true meaning of conversion—not that every person will experience such a dramatic conversion. (I did not.) Conversion to a life through the resurrected Christ, however, must involve deep changes within one's life and lifestyle. Any Christian should eventually see some of the significant changes God is trying to bring about in his or her life.

The biggest change for Paul came in his attitude toward the law of Moses. He had not been a typical Jew who was careful only about a few key laws such as the circumcision and food laws. Paul tried to follow *all* the laws, and he believed that he had succeeded! When he discovered that his pursuit of law-based righteousness had led him to oppose God, Paul's attitude toward the law changed radically. Because of his past history, he wrestled more extensively and profoundly with the issue of the law than anyone else.

Finally, note that Paul was quite willing to tell his own story (his personal testimony) to help explain the gospel to others. In our time, personal testimonies are sometimes selfishly misused as vehicles to display one's own personal triumphs, but telling others what God has done in your own life is a powerful way to share your faith with others. Whether the listeners are unbelievers or, as in this case, believers struggling with their faith, they can be encouraged by your story. When you tell others about the differences God has made in your life, and especially when they can see those differences lived out in your life, your testimony can become just the "good news" that people need to hear.

Questions for Discussion

1. If you have accepted Christ as savior, what was your life like before you became a Christian? How is it different today?

2. Was your conversion dramatic, like Paul's, or more gradual? What were the significant factors that led to your decision?

3. How will a knowledge of early Christian history, and especially knowledge of Paul's earlier life, help us understand Galatians more accurately?

4. How difficult do you think it was for Peter, James, and John—all Jewish Christians—to admit Gentile Christians into the church? Why?

5. With what group of people have you previously had the most difficulty associating (blacks, whites, poor, farmers, Hispanics, wealthy)? Do you think God might ever want you to work with that group of people?

6. How can you use your personal testimony to encourage others in their faith?

Note

[1]The James mentioned in Galatians was the brother of Jesus. He should not be confused with James the son of Zebedee, brother of John, and member of Jesus' band of twelve disciples. That James was martyred by King Herod in Acts 12:2.

Chapter 3

Justification by Faith

Galatians 2:11–21

Even church members who know little about Paul usually know the one phrase, "justification by faith." This is a doctrine that lies close to the heart of the Christian faith, one over which Luther launched the Reformation. In this chapter we will review the passage where the doctrine of justification by faith was first explained.

In his massive commentary on Galatians, Hans Dieter Betz drew attention to Paul's use of Greek rhetorical principles in his composition of the letter. The most important part of the letter was the "proposition" or thesis statement[1] in 2:15-21. Here we find Paul's thesis—that salvation comes not through works of the law but by faith. Paul filled the next two chapters of his letter with various arguments in support of his thesis.

Comment

11-12 Paul recounted an event that occurred sometime after the Jerusalem conference described in 2:1-10. Unfortunately, this experience was not nearly so positive. At this point Paul had returned to Antioch, the mother church for the Gentile mission. Peter (called by his Aramaic name, "Cephas") came for a visit. At first he not only tolerated the law-free gospel for Gentiles but participated in law-free living himself. Sitting with Gentile Christians seems insignificant to us, but for a first-century Jew it meant discarding the detailed food restrictions found both in scripture and in the rabbis' oral traditions about scripture. Gentiles ate pork and other unclean food; to eat with them was to become unclean oneself, but at first Peter was quite happy to enjoy meals with the Gentile Christians. That is consistent with the account of Peter's dream in which God told Peter that all foods were to be considered "clean" or acceptable to eat (Acts 10:10-35).

James, who was still in Jerusalem, sent a message to Peter that caused him to change his behavior. Apparently, James and Peter both feared the wrath of a group that Paul simply called "the circumcision." The NRSV translates this phrase as "the circumcision faction," which would suggest that James and Peter were afraid of Jewish Christians who insisted that keeping the Jewish law was essential for all Christians. This is certainly a plausible explanation, but an second equally plausible explanation would be to translate the phrase as simply "the Jews." Paul used the term, "the circumcised," to refer to non-Christian Jews in 2:7-9, so it seems reasonable to assume such a reference in verses 11-12. In this case, we should picture James and Peter breaking contact with Gentiles so as not to antagonize non-Christian Jews. Their motive was perhaps more pragmatic than theological. They were understandably trying to avoid bringing the wrath of the larger Jewish population upon the much smaller group of Jewish Christian churches.

13-14 Paul did not care who James and Peter were afraid of offending. Even when Paul's fellow missionary Barnabas backed away from the Gentile Christians, Paul refused to back down from his theological convictions. In fact, he attacked the inconsistent behavior of Peter and Barnabas as "hypocrisy"! The Greek word he used is a compound of the verb, *hupokrinomai*, from which we get our word "hypocrite." Paul saw clearly the dangers of such hypocrisy. If salvation was proclaimed to the Gentiles on the basis of faith in Christ, but Gentile converts discovered that they were still not acceptable dinner companions for Jewish Christians, then few Gentiles would be interested. How great could a purported "salvation" be if it only granted second-class status?

Paul's firm stand at Antioch was one of the great turning points in Christian history. Perhaps the only comparable incident was Luther's famous "Here I stand" speech that launched the Reformation. If Paul had lost his nerve and given in to James, Peter, and Barnabas, the Christian movement might never have spread throughout the Roman world. Whatever faults Paul had, however, timidity was not one of them. The principle of law-free salvation for the Gentiles, which Paul had politely advocated in Jerusalem, he aggressively defended in Antioch. He recounted the incident to the Galatians because he saw that the same principle—a law-free salvation—was threatened in Galatia just as it had been threatened at an earlier time in Antioch.

15 After finishing his autobiographical sketch, Paul drew the theological conclusion to which the entire narrative has been pointing. He did not want to be perceived as anti-Jewish. In fact, even as a Christian he still considered himself to be a Jew. Furthermore, he believed that Jews were generally less sinful than Gentiles who did not have God's law to guide them.

16 Verse 16 is one of the great verses of the entire Bible, deserving as much recognition as John 3:16. Paul explained his understanding of salvation, using a forensic metaphor drawn from a first-century courtroom. Picture yourself as the accused person in that courtroom. The charges against you are read. How will you defend yourself? On what basis do you hope to have the judge declare you "righteous" or—to use modern terminology—"not guilty"?

Before his conversion, Paul would probably have based his hope for justification on two factors: (1) his status as a member of God's covenant people and (2) his performance of "works of the law." As mentioned in the introduction, we need to correct a common misconception of ancient Judaism at this point. Christian scholars have often portrayed first-century Judaism as a religion based on salvation by works. The ancient Jews believed they *earned* salvation by virtue of their obedience to the law—a religion of works, not of grace. The Jews were legalists, according to many Christians.

E. P. Sanders, in his groundbreaking work, *Paul and Palestinian Judaism*, however, has demonstrated that this is not a fair description of first-century Judaism. Most Jews were aware of grace; God had shown grace to the Jewish people by means of his covenant with them. They believed that their careful obedience to God's laws constituted their proper response to the grace God showed them in making the covenant with Moses. They did not earn salvation by obeying the law, but obedience was required. As Sanders puts it, obedience to the law was not the way you "got in" (as a member of God's elect), but it was rather the way you "stayed in."

Some of the strictest Pharisees, such as the preconversion Paul, put tremendous emphasis upon "works of the law." While the less dedicated Jews thought it enough to observe circumcision, honor the Sabbath, and follow the food laws, Paul insisted that every regulation of the law be obeyed. He clearly felt that his obedience made him "righteous" before God. (Some of the Pharisees who battled with Jesus obviously felt the same way.) When he met the resurrected Christ, Paul was shown how sinful he really was. He experienced the grace of forgiveness and found that he could only stand before God on the basis of faith in Jesus Christ.

Paul concluded that if he, the strictest Pharisee he knew, was not justified by works of the law, then no one was justified on that basis. The beauty of his discovery was that justification or salvation was a possibility for every person. Rare was the Gentile who could even have approached Paul's level of obedience to the law of Moses. Few were even interested in the attempt, but finding a savior was already an interest of many Gentiles, and Paul could show them the way to find and follow that savior.

The NRSV and NIV both give the traditional translation of verse 16—that one is justified "through *faith in* Jesus Christ." Yet many scholars correctly point out that the phrase may be translated, "through the *faithfulness of* Jesus Christ." The Greek phrase allows either meaning, and perhaps Paul intended both. Certainly Paul did want to give as much emphasis to Christ's role in our salvation as he did to the importance of our faith in Christ.

17 Although verse 17 is rather confusing, it probably reflects the objections of Paul's opponents, the Judaizers, who were wooing the Galatians away from a Pauline version of Christianity. Likely these opponents attacked justification by faith with an argument like this: "Paul's denial of the validity of the law of Moses for Gentiles has allowed some of these Galatian Christians to slip back into a very sinful lifestyle. They are found to be sinners. So faith in Christ, without the support of the law, encourages people to sin. This makes Christ a servant of sin!" Paul agreed that Gentile Christians were sinners, but Jews were sinners too. Demanding obedience to the law would not change either fact. Faith in Christ did not encourage sin, for Christ was certainly not a servant of sin.

18 Although Paul used "I" in verse 18, he really had the example of Peter and Barnabas in mind. Paul meant that when a Christian accepted justification by faith in Christ and accepted Gentiles on the basis of their faith in Christ, then he or she had torn down the law. After that was done, one could not possibly "rebuild" the law as Peter and Barnabas did when they reverted to their former lifestyle and stopped eating meals with Gentile Christians. This was the true transgression, because it defeated God's purpose in sending Christ.

19-20 Paul waxed eloquent about being crucified with Christ. What precisely did he mean, though? How could he say that "through the law" he died "to the law"?

Most likely Paul meant that the purpose of the law was to lead to Christ's death on the cross. This is confirmed when he quoted Deuteronomy 21:23, a verse *from the law* (see Gal 3:13). Paul interpreted that verse to mean that Christ became a curse for us by dying on the cross.[2] Christ's death brought to an end the need for the law, so in this sense the law points to its own end, and as the believer mysteriously participates in Christ's death, he or she "dies" to the law. That is, he or she has no more relation to the law. If our reading is correct, then Paul meant roughly that the law led to Christ's death, which in turn ended the need for the law, and thus freed believers from the law's demands.

Paul switched metaphors for salvation. Whereas the term "justification" created courtroom images, Paul shifted to a more mystical image of mutual indwelling. More than a hundred times in his letters Paul referred to the Christian as being "in Christ," but in verses 19-20 he described the photo negative of that image—"Christ . . . lives in me." The meaning is essentially the same. Christ did not die simply to free people from the law so they could wander in any direction they desired. He died so that people could freely choose to allow his spirit to enter their lives and give them direction. That, according to Paul, happens when one trusts in Christ. The old self dies and Christ comes to live in the life of the believer. The booklet, "My Heart, Christ's Home," which has been popular on college campuses, may seem a bit unsophisticated, but it gets fairly close to Paul's meaning.

21 Peter and Barnabas came close to returning to life under the law in Antioch, and the Judaizers in Galatia wanted to do the same. This choice amounted to a nullification of the grace God offered through Christ's death. Paul's profound challenge to the Judaizers stood unanswered: "If justification comes through the law, then Christ died for nothing." Remember, however, that Paul did not arrive at this conclusion immediately after Christ's crucifixion. Only after his experience with the resurrected Christ did Paul change his entire perspective on the meaning of the crucifixion.

Theological Reflection

Perhaps the most practical lesson that Christians can learn from Galatians 2:11-21 is to ask themselves the question: "What theology does my behavior suggest?" Paul attacked the hypocrisy of Peter and Barnabas and drew a crucial theological point from the incident. He saw that by refusing to eat with the Gentiles, Jewish Christians were undercutting their own message of salvation through Christ. Even while separating from the Gentile Christians, Peter and Barnabas would undoubtedly still have *said* that the Gentile Christians were saved, but their *behavior* communicated a different message.

If faith in Christ only brought with it second class status, by inference he must have been only a second-class savior! Do we send the same message when we refuse to invite a new co-worker to our church because he or she is of another race? "Their family probably wouldn't feel comfortable at our Wednesday night supper," sounds like an excuse that Peter or Barnabas may have used. But you know what Paul would have said!

Reading Galatians can easily give the impression that Paul was inflexible and unyielding about every issue. We know from Romans and 1 Corinthians, however, that he was willing to grant concessions and compromise on various issues that he did not consider to be of vital theological importance (such as questions about the proper day to worship or the appropriateness of eating meat that had been sacrificed to idols). We are not surprised to find that the crucifixion and resurrection were two theological doctrines that Paul would not compromise.

Notice that Paul also considered *fellowship within the church* to be one of his theological non-negotiables. If the early church was to offer Christ as a savior to all people—devout Jews, immoral Gentiles, wealthy women, drunks, city officials, thieves, tentmakers, homosexuals, and physicians—then the church had to show that all these diverse people were accepted on an equal basis. Some of their behavior had to change, no doubt, but Christ had died for them all equally. Before God, and thus within the fellowship of the church, they all stood shoulder to shoulder. No person was above another.

How successful are our churches today in maintaining this principle? Are blue collar workers equal to their supervisors in your congregation? Can a housewife be chosen to chair a crucial committee even if her husband does not have a prestigious career? Will a visiting corporal from a nearby army base be greeted as enthusiastically as his base commander? For Paul, whatever "status" one had was surrendered in exchange for the "status" of being justified in Christ. Then, as now, some people had a hard time giving up their hard-earned prestige.

Paul himself would never have given up his "status" as a righteous, law-obeying Pharisee if not for his experience with the risen Christ. Only then could he see that no one, not even Paul, could stand righteous before God on the basis of his works of the law. Righteousness, or justification, is only possible through a person's faith in Christ. Paul would probably also agree with the translation of 2:16 that we are "justified by the *faithfulness of* Christ."

Questions for Discussion

1. Before reading Galatians, what did you know about justification by faith?

2. Were you taught by your parents not to eat meals with any particular group of people? How did that experience help you understand the opposition some Jewish Christians raised to allowing Gentile and Jewish Christians to eat meals together?

3. Have you ever defended your beliefs in a situation where everyone else seemed to oppose you? How difficult was it to stand your ground?

4. Have you ever thought, "Christ lives in me"? How might that awareness change your behavior?

5. Consider the meaning of the phrase, "justified by faith in Christ." Now compare the meaning of the alternative translation, "justified by the faithfulness of Christ."

Notes

[1] Hans Dieter Betz, *Galatians*, Hermenia (Philadelphia: Fortress, 1979) 113-27.
[2] Traditional Jewish interpretation equated death on a tree with death on a wooden cross.

Chapter 4

Before Moses Came Abraham

Galatians 3:1–18

After Paul stated his proposition or thesis quite forcefully, he needed to back up his claim that salvation did not come through works of the law but by faith in Christ. To support his claim he launched a series of loosely connected arguments, three of which are found in Galatians 3:1-18:

> The Galatians already received the Spirit (vv. 1-5)
> Abraham was justified by faith (vv. 6-14)
> Abraham preceded Moses (vv. 15-18)

Paul's arguments actually continue past 3:18, but since most of this section deals with arguments involving Abraham, it will be convenient to consider 3:1-18 at one time.

Baptists, and indeed most Protestants, take the concept of justification by faith for granted. We have been so influenced by Paul's version of Christianity that we hardly think justification by faith needs any defense. Was it not obvious to every Christian that salvation came through faith alone? The answer is "no." Let us consider for a moment how difficult it was for Paul to make his case.

All the early Christians, including Paul and his opponents in Galatia, agreed that Jesus was the messiah, the

Christ. They also agreed that the books we now call the "Old Testament" were scripture—God's written message to his people. The books that later were collected into what we call the "New Testament" had not yet been written, so the only Bible the early Christians had was the Old Testament. The Old Testament certainly emphasized the importance of following God's law. Many Jews saw Moses as the most crucial figure in scripture and thought that God's giving of the law to Moses at Mount Sinai was perhaps the most important of God's miracles.

When law-honoring Jews accepted Jesus as the promised messiah, most of them did not see any reason to abandon the law. They probably heard how Jesus himself had criticized the Pharisees for their overly strict interpretation of the law. But this seemed only to prohibit Christians from taking an overly strict view of the law; it did not bring the law to an end. Only as significant numbers of Gentiles were converted, did the deep theological question become clear. Should Gentile converts to Christ be required to follow the Jewish law, or at least the most important parts of that law? Many Jewish Christians answered "yes," but Paul said "no!" He was trying to convince the Gentile Christians in Galatia not to submit to the very law he had been taught to honor.

Comment

1 Paul was not a diplomat! He let his emotions flow freely through his pen (in this case, through his scribe's pen). His exasperation with the Galatians is evident as he addressed them directly for the first time since chapter one—"you foolish Galatians!" It would be interesting to know how the readers reacted to being called "foolish." Did some of them react angrily and side even more strongly with Paul's opponents? Or did Paul's stern words shock the Galatians and cause them to realize the truth of what Paul was saying?

His rhetorical question was not meant to be answered. Paul showed no real interest in the names of his opponents in Galatia; his real concern was that the members of his former congregation would realize that they had been "bewitched," and that this realization would help them break the spell.

What did Paul mean when he said that Christ had been "publicly exhibited as crucified"? Most commentators assert that Paul was referring to the sermons he had preached to the Galatians about Christ's death on the cross. Conceivably, a poster or drawing of the crucified Christ might have been exhibited in one of the homes where the Galatians worshiped.

2 Paul asked a question that he really wanted the Galatians to answer. He reminded them that they had received the Holy Spirit and cleverly asked if they first received the Spirit because of obedience to the law. Of course, Paul knew that the Galatians received the Spirit after professing faith in Jesus because he was there when they made their profession of faith. (His readers knew that, too.) The point is that God's sending of the spirit into the lives of those Galatian believers was evidence that they had already been justified by their faith. Before they even thought about obeying the law of Moses they had already been justified before God, and the Spirit was God's seal of approval of their faith.

3-4 Paul's basic argument was really quite similar to the one the angel Clarence used on George Bailey (played by Jimmy Stewart) in the classic movie, *It's a Wonderful Life*. Why are you so dissatisfied with what you already have? Can you not see all the good things God has already done for you and through you? We are only left to wonder if Paul was as successful as Clarence. Did his argument convince the Galatians that because they had received the Spirit they already had a wonderful life and thus did not need the changes that obedience to the law would bring?

5 How did the Galatians *know* they had received the Holy Spirit? They knew it experientially. More specifically, they had seen miracles worked by the Spirit. One such miracle may have been the healing of a man crippled from birth, worked by the Spirit through Paul when he was preaching in Lystra, a city of Galatia. (Read Acts 14:8-20 for the details.) Other miracles may have been worked through the Galatians themselves. The point is that Paul presented more evidence for which the Galatians themselves were witnesses—evidence that proved they had already received the Holy Spirit—so Paul concluded his first argument in favor of justification by faith rather than works of the law. Because they had faith, God justified the Gentiles and sent the Spirit as proof that God had accepted them. This all happened without any concern for the law of Moses. Therefore, the law was not necessary for Gentiles at all.

6 Paul's second argument in support of his thesis was a more objective one, based on scripture and history. Whereas his first argument was based on an appeal fo the Galatians' subjective experience of the Spirit, the second argument turned to Abraham.

Abraham was well-known, even to Gentiles, as the father of the Jewish people. No doubt the Judaizers had

Gal. 3:1–18 Before Moses Came Abraham

appealed to Abraham as the one through whom God had introduced circumcision (Gen 17:9-14). Paul did not dispute this. Rather, he sought to prove that Abraham was first of all a person of faith.

Recall Abraham's story. God had made three promises as part of his covenant with Abraham (Gen 12:1-3; 15:1-21). He promised that Abraham would (1) inhabit the Promised Land, (2) become the father of a great nation, and (3) be the conduit for God's blessing to all nations.

After inhabiting the promised land of Canaan, Abraham reflected on his chances of becoming the father of a great nation. The odds against such seemed great. He and his wife Sarah were already very old and had no children. One night God showed Abraham the countless stars in the night sky and promised him that his descendants would be just as numerous. Abraham "believed God, and it was reckoned to him as righteousness," as Paul quoted Genesis 15:6.

Paul based his entire understanding of God's plan of salvation on this key verse. God made a promise, and Abraham believed or trusted in God to fulfill that promise. Therefore, Abraham was first a person of faith, and God responded to Abraham's faith by "reckoning" or judging him to be righteous. The Greek noun *dikaiosune* is translated "righteousness," and the verbal form of the same word means "declared righteous" or "justified." Thus, concluded Paul, Abraham was justified by faith.

7 Paul then applied Abraham's example to the situation in Galatia. The Judaizers had no doubt claimed that descendants of Abraham were those who followed his example and were circumcised (or in the case of women, those who had their sons circumcised). For centuries, virtually all Jews had held this same viewpoint, but Paul countered their claim, insisting that the true children of

Abraham were those who believed or trusted in God as Abraham did.

Paul did not voice his assumption that the object of this faith was no longer just God. True faith includes trust in Jesus as God's messiah or Christ. Paul could make this silent assumption because, on this point, the Judaizers agreed with him.

8-9 The first two promises that God made to Abraham had received great emphasis throughout Jewish history. One could easily read the entire Old Testament as a story of God's fulfillment of his promises to give the Promised Land to Abraham's descendants and then shape those descendants into a great nation. God's third promise to Abraham had received relatively little attention. Paul declared that the third promise had been fulfilled in God's justification of the Gentiles (or nations) by faith. Those Gentiles who believed in Christ received the ultimate blessing, salvation or justification, because they had believed just as Abraham did.

10 Paul's opponents agreed that faith in Christ was a wonderful thing for the Gentiles. They simply wanted to make the believing Gentiles obey the law of Moses. Almost certainly they quoted Deuteronomy 27:26 to the effect that the law must be obeyed, or else one would be under God's curse, but Paul turned that verse against them. He claimed that the verse did not call for obedience to a few "important" laws like circumcision, food laws, and Sabbath observance, but it called down a curse unless one observed *all* the laws. Remember, before his conversion Paul followed the law more closely than anyone he knew. Daily he saw Jews who followed some or most of the laws but fell short of Paul's own high standard of obedience. He had spotted their transgressions as only a legalist could! The ex-legalist refused to allow people to be graded on a curve. Everyone who followed the law less rigorously than Paul had in his pre-conversion days fell under the curse of Deuteronomy 27:26. (Paul had also fallen under the curse because he had persecuted the messiah.)

11 Using a quotation from Habakkuk 2:4, Paul set up faith and law as two different paths to righteousness, only one of which could be the correct path. The two routes could not be combined. The scripture quotation demonstrated once again that righteousness came via faith.

12 Paul quoted yet another verse of scripture (Lev 18:5) is quoted to show that the law and faith were two mutually incompatible choices. Some interpreters, hoping to rescue the law from oblivion, have suggested that Paul was not actually attacking the law, but only attacking an extreme and unhealthy reliance upon the law. Stephen Westerholm, in his remarkably clear study of Paul and the law, refutes that opinion. He notes that the Greek word (*nomos*) is used both here and in 3:10, where it definitely refers to the law of Moses. Likely Paul referred to the law of Moses in 3:12 as well.[1] Paul attacked not only an extreme reliance upon the law—but *any* reliance upon the law. Verse 11 describes the right choice—living by faith—and verse 12 describes the wrong choice—doing works of the law.

13 Verse 13 is one of the Bible's most shocking verses, rivaled only by Jesus' words from the cross, "My God, My God, why have you forsaken me?" (Mark 15:34).

Deuteronomy 21:23, "Cursed is everyone who hangs on a tree," had for years been understood to refer to crucifixion on a cross (tree). Jews believed that God cursed anyone who had committed a crime so heinous that the Romans crucified him. Most Americans feel the same about our death row inmates—they deserve to be cursed by God!

Before his conversion, Paul surely quoted Deuteronomy 21:23 to prove that Jesus could not have been the messiah since he was crucified and, therefore, cursed by God. As a Christian, Paul ironically maintained the same belief . . . with a twist. Christ was indeed cursed, but on our behalf and in our place. Both Gentiles and Jews, even the strictest Jews, fell under the curse of Deuteronomy 27:26 for not obeying all the laws, but on the cross Christ took that curse upon himself. This is what Paul meant by redemption.

14 Bringing his argument to a conclusion, Paul explained that this must have been God's plan when God first promised Abraham that the Gentiles would be blessed through him. The messiah was sent and took the penalty deserved by Jews and Gentiles. This substitutionary act opened the way for justification of all Jews and Gentiles who believed in God's promised messiah. They trusted in God, just as Abraham had when the promise was made.

15 Paul's third argument in support of his thesis connected an example from daily life with his own reading of Old Testament history. A key term in 3:15-18 is *diatheke*, which means both "a will" and "a covenant." Paul's first point is refreshingly easy to grasp: Once a person's will is ratified, it is binding and cannot be changed. Whoever is supposed to inherit something will inherit exactly that.

16 God's promises to Abraham had traditionally been claimed by the Jewish people as their own, but Paul re-read the will and discovered that the inheritance was not promised to all of the physical descendants of Abraham, the "seeds"[2] or Jewish people. Rather, it was promised to the true descendent or "seed" of Abraham, Jesus Christ.

17 Verse 17 is the key to Paul's third argument. Although Moses is never explicitly mentioned in Galatians, his shadow frequently darkens the pages of Paul's letter.

Moses, the lawgiver, was certainly the hero of every Jew who honored the law—and that included the Judaizers who opposed Paul in Galatia. Their claim had to be carefully answered by Paul, for he certainly did not want to say anything against Moses. Some response had to be given, so Paul answered from history.

Long before God gave the law to Moses (430 years before), God made promises to Abraham as part of a covenant with him, and that covenant was still valid. Through that covenant God's promises were inherited by the true seed—Christ who, through his death, made the promises available to anyone who had faith in him.

18 To claim, as the Judaizers did, that the inheritance came through the law, implied that God's will or covenant had changed from the time it was first made with Abraham, but Paul insisted that God's promises to Abraham were still valid.

Theological Reflection

The success of the charismatic movement during the last three decades has made most Baptists afraid to say much about the Holy Spirit. Clearly, Paul thought that a Christian who has been justified by faith has also received the Spirit and should be able to recognize the Spirit's work. Few of us have seen the Spirit work miracles in our lives, but are we truly aware of the Spirit's voice leading us from within? When difficulties arise and we doubt our salvation (which was basically what was happening to the Galatians), we first need to be able to recall the personal, subjective experience we have already had with God.

That subjective experience needs to be supplemented by an objective knowledge of scripture. Paul quoted or paraphrased the Old Testament eight times in these eighteen verses of Galatians. He obviously held a high view of the authority of scripture. Perhaps Paul's example can be especially helpful to moderate Baptists today. Paul's opponents were attacking him by citing scripture about the importance of obeying the law. He could easily have decided to argue only from personal experience and de-emphasize the importance of scripture, but he refused to surrender the Bible to those who were attacking him. In the same way, moderate Baptists today must not de-emphasize the Bible just because fundamentalists use it to attack us. We must not respond by closing our Bibles or putting them on the shelf, but rather by reading them more thoroughly and interpreting them more faithfully.

Baptists, in particular, have no real place to stand apart from the Bible. When John Smyth and Thomas Helwys formed the first Baptist church, their intent was not to "become Baptists," but rather to found a congregation whose life and thought was based on the Bible. They wanted to become "biblical Christians." Today Baptists can learn much from other Christian denominations, but if we wish to contribute anything unique to the larger church, it will surely be drawn from a closer study, clearer interpretation, and more profound application of God's written word.

Finally, what can we say about the law and legalism today? Some of you think I have been too hard on the law because you like the Ten Commandments and think our society would be better off if more people followed them. I basically agree with you! My job in this commentary, however, is to give an honest interpretation of what Paul wrote, not to change it. Furthermore, Paul was writing for

Christians, not for society as a whole. If he took away the comforting guidance of the law with one hand, he gave a better guide with the other hand (as you will see in Gal 5).

Others of you are already so influenced by Paul that your only difficulty is wondering why the Galatians ever considered submitting to the law. You are comfortable with jokes about the legalism at Jerry Falwell's Liberty University, and it seems incredible to you that anyone would ever find that lifestyle attractive.

Consider your local Mennonite community. (If you do not know any Mennonites, rent the video of the powerful movie, *The Witness*, and see Harrison Ford play a tough Philadelphia cop who develops a deep appreciation for the community structure and high ethical standards of the Amish people, the strictest Mennonites. Compared with the anarchy, violence, and immorality he is used to, Ford finds the Amish lifestyle very appealing.)

The Galatian Christians found themselves in a similar situation. Immersed in an immoral, libertine culture, they were easily swayed by the Judaizers' appeal to come under the protection of the Jewish law. The law could provide structure, community, and morality. It could be simply added to faith in Christ, which they already had. They hesitated—the offer sounded good. No wonder Paul found it necessary to use many arguments to keep the Galatian Christians from adopting a law-based lifestyle.

Questions for Discussion

1. Have you received the Holy Spirit in your life? If so, what results have you seen from this experience?

2. When you think of "faith," do you normally think in terms of intellectual content—what you believe? Or do you think of faith as more of a personal trust in Christ? Does either connotation of faith give greater insight into Abraham's experience with God?

3. Do you find it hard to believe that Christ "became a curse for us"? How do you understand the deeper significance of the crucifixion?

4. Are you one who wishes the Ten Commandments were more widely followed today? Or are you a person prone to tell jokes about legalists? If you had been a member of the Galatian church, how would you have felt about Paul's letter so far?

5. What do you think about the Amish lifestyle? Is legalism always bad?

Notes

[1] Steven Westerholm, *Israel's Law and the Church's Faith* (Grand Rapids MI: Eerdmans, 1988) 131.

[2] The NIV gives the literal reading of "seeds," while the NRSV gives the translation, "offsprings."

Chapter 5

Why Give the Law If You Don't Want Legalism?

Galatians 3:19–4:11

Paul's opponents were no dummies. They were not about to remain silent while his letter was read to the Galatian congregations. They would have their own arguments ready for a counterattack against Paul as soon as the letter was finished. For this reason Paul needed to anticipate what their counter-arguments might be and answer them within his letter. One can almost hear the Judaizers thinking: "O.K., so Abraham did have faith centuries before Moses received the law on Mount Sinai, but God still gave the law! Why did God give the law if God did not want us to follow it?" Paul anticipated that exact question and gave his answer in 3:19-4:7. He set out to show why God gave the law and how the situation had changed after the messiah's coming.

Comment

19 Paul stole the very question from the lips of his opponents. He gave one obvious answer to which all will agree—the law was given because of sins or transgressions—but then he added two qualifiers. The first qualifier is the most significant—the little word, "until." The law was given and had a purpose *until* the "offspring" or "seed" arrived. Of course, that offspring, Christ, had come, but Paul delayed further discussion of this key point until 3:23-26.

He added an obscure comment that the law was "ordained through angels by a mediator." Paul tried to explain what he meant by adding verse 20, but this only further adds to our confusion. What was Paul talking about?

20 He was apparently referring to a Jewish belief that angels participated in God's giving of the law to Moses on Mount Sinai. That tradition was probably based on Deuteronomy 33:2: "With him were myriads of holy ones." The term "mediator" probably refers to Moses himself. Even with these insights we are still left confused. Numerous interpretations have been offered, so certainty is not possible.

Perhaps Richard Longenecker, in his outstanding commentary on Galatians, has offered the most plausible explanation. According to Longenecker, Paul was showing yet another weakness of the Mosaic law. It was not delivered directly from the one God to God's people (as God delivered the promise to Abraham), but came via the surrounding angels and through Moses as a mediator. Apparently the involvement of angels and a mediator showed a weakness in the law.[1] This is the least convincing argument in Paul's arsenal.

21 Paul earlier drew a contrast between the promises, which were made to Abraham, and the law, which was given through Moses, but in this verse he warned against pushing this contrast too far. There was no contradiction where God first made promises to Abraham and later gave the law through Moses. In both cases God was interested in making the people righteous. The law was given with that goal in mind, but the law was not able to achieve that goal. Paul used a contrary-to-fact conditional sentence to clearly demonstrate that the law was never able to impart righteousness. If the law could have made anyone righteous, it would have done so for Paul. He had traveled down that path as far as anyone could, and he knew it did not lead to righteousness.

22 By "scripture," Paul probably had in mind Deuteronomy 27:26 (reread his quotation of that verse in Gal 3:10) and other similar verses that called for a penalty upon those who broke the law. Scripture hemmed in or imprisoned everyone by pointing out individual sins and the power of sin in general. Thus, the need for redemption was obvious.

23-24 Paul shifted to a new image for the law—a *paidagogos* (translated by the term, "disciplinarian," in the NRSV, and by the phrase, "put in charge," in the NIV). The *paidagogos* was a household slave used by the ancient Greeks to watch over their preschool children. He taught basic skills such as manners and letter shapes, but when the children were ready for school the *paidagogos* took them to a real teacher (therefore the KJV translation of "schoolmaster" for the *paidagogos* is quite misleading). We have no exact equivalent in America; perhaps a stern British nanny is the closest modern equivalent. Like a nanny, the slave performed a necessary task, but one that was preparatory and temporary.

The meaning of this illustration is clear. The law was necessary and its purpose was good in its time, but its task was finished. The children had been turned over to the master-teacher, Jesus Christ, and had no need of returning to the supervision of the *paidagogos*.

25-26 The age of law ended, and the age of faith began with the coming of Christ Jesus. Previously Paul spoke of Abraham's faith or trust in God. When he said that "faith has come," he referred to a more specific form of faith—faith in Jesus as the Christ. This faith in Christ was the one that justified, although in Abraham's day justification came to those who had faith in God without any knowledge of the messiah.

Faith in Christ came during Paul's lifetime, and he left the care of the *paidagogos* to be tutored by Christ. Did he intend that every Christian should go through that same sequence—first under the law and then coming to faith? Unfortunately, Paul left that question unanswered.

27 Having contrasted the law with faith in Christ, Paul shifted his attention to the effects of faith upon the believer. Take note that Paul assumed that true children of faith will be part of a church (he was writing to churches) and that those who profess faith in Christ will be baptized into Christ. Paul did not even consider that converts might try to dispense with membership in a congregation and ordinances such as baptism. Perhaps televangelism had not yet reached Galatia!

When Paul added that believers have "clothed" themselves with Christ, he meant that they have taken on Christ's characteristics—they are becoming like him. While

Christians are free from the law, they are not free from Christ. They are to be like him.

28 Because the role of women has become such a hotly debated topic in our churches and American society, verse 28 has become the most widely quoted verse in the entire Galatian letter. Note first that Paul was not directly discussing women's roles but rather describing the life in Christ that was available to any who professed faith. His primary interest was obviously the relationship between Jews and Greeks. Paul still called himself a Jew (Gal 2:15), but because God had offered justification to everyone in the same manner (by faith), the distinction between Jews and Gentiles was essentially meaningless. The common experience of faith in Christ so overshadowed everything else about a Christian's life that all other distinctions faded into oblivion.

All of Paul's arguments to this effect remind us that many people did not accept his viewpoint easily. To be part of a group that brought Jews and Gentiles together as brothers and sisters was a culturally shattering experience. Just as shocking was the thought that slaves would be accepted on an equal basis with freeborn people. Again, Paul knew that slavery still existed. He did not demand its immediate abolition, but clearly taught that faith in Christ made the slave/free distinction meaningless. Although Christians did not abolish slavery for about 1800 years, Paul planted the seeds for abolition here in his letter to the Galatians.

Likewise, Paul did not insist that all cultural distinctions between men and women be abolished. He did, however, adopt the radical viewpoint that the universally maintained distinction between the status of men and women counted for nothing when compared with the common experience of faith in Christ. This seed has taken about 2000 years to bloom. No wonder Paul's churches were so attractive to Gentiles, slaves, and women. There they found acceptance before God on an equal basis with everyone else and experienced being "one in Christ."

29 Verse 29 recalls the earlier discussion of Abraham's "seed" or "offspring" found in 3:16. In that verse Paul insisted that God's promises to Abraham were also given to Christ as the true seed of Abraham. He added that the promises were extended through Christ to all who believed in him, making them heirs of God's promises.

4:1-2 Paul returned to the language of inheritance and developed that image more fully. Heirs had little freedom while they were children (minors). They were told what to do in much the same way as slaves were given orders, but that changed once the date of actual inheritance set by the father arrived. After that decisive date the heirs had far more freedom than when they answered to guardians and trustees.

3 One could easily guess how Paul would apply this analogy: "So with us, while we were minors, we were enslaved to the law." Instead of "law," Paul substituted the phrase, "the *stoicheia* of the world." What did he mean? The exact meaning of the phrase is hotly debated. The two most likely options are reflected in the NRSV translation, "elemental spirits," and the NIV, "basic principles." In this case, the context seems to favor the NIV's translation.

Paul and his readers were at one time enslaved to the "basic principles of the world." For Paul and any Jewish Christian readers of his letter, those "basic principles" certainly included the Mosaic Law. For them, Paul said what we would expect—Jews were enslaved to the law. For the Gentile readers, the same phrase would bring a different thought to mind. They, too, were enslaved to basic principles, but in their case the basic principles were the various pagan myths and cults to which they had given allegiance before converting to Christ. By saying that, "while we were minors, we were enslaved to the basic principles of the world," Paul was able to show readers of both Jewish and Gentile heritage that they had been enslaved and in need of redemption.

4-5 God took the initiative and sent the Son to redeem, or buy back, both Jews and Gentiles who had previously been enslaved. Let your imagination take you back to the antebellum days of the Old South. Picture an auction block with slaves standing upon it. They do not own themselves so are for sale to the highest bidder. Listen as Christ calls out the highest bid and purchases the slaves. They have been *redeemed.*

Verses 4 and 5 contain one of the earliest Christian confessions about Christ. Paul told us that Jesus was God's Son, that God sent him to earth, that he was fully human (born of a woman), and that he was Jewish (born under the law). Surprisingly, Paul said nothing about a virgin birth. He either had not heard the story that we read today in Matthew and Luke (remember that none of the gospels had yet been written), or he knew the story but decided against mentioning it here.

Already Paul had shifted from the image of an heir receiving an inheritance to one of a slave being redeemed. He shifted again to a third picture, one of an orphan being adopted. All three images were united, however, in conveying the dramatic change in status that the key event would bring. Inheritance, redemption, and adoption were all descriptions of the experience that followed a commitment of faith in Christ.

6-7 The Galatians had already experienced this faith in Christ and subsequent change in status before God. Paul reminded them that the Spirit (the "Spirit of his Son" is the Holy Spirit) had brought that awareness to them through the ecstatic cry, "Abba. Father!" The term *Abba* ("Daddy") was the Aramaic word used by children for their fathers. It was shocking to address God this way, acceptable only because Jesus had done so himself (when he prayed in the Garden of Gethsemane, Mark 14:36). In fact, as far as we know, Jesus was the first to address God in such an intensely personal way, but because the Galatians believed in Christ and became children of God, they too could call out to God as their *Abba*.

8-9 Before their conversion to Christ, the Galatians had worshipped various pagan deities. These idols, and worship of them, formed the basic principles of pagan religious life. The Galatians had been enslaved to them. The Galatians turned once again to "weak and miserable principles" (using the NIV translation, which is preferable at this point to the NRSV). They actually turned to a different religious principle—the Jewish law—than they served before. From Paul's perspective, however, slavery to pagan deities or slavery to the Jewish law were both miserable choices compared to the freedom that came through faith in Christ.

10-11 Previously Paul had mentioned circumcision and food laws as specific examples of legal requirements the Judaizers pushed. He added calendar requirements to that list. To please the Judaizers, the Galatians began to observe the Jewish Sabbath and special holy days such as the Feast of Tabernacles or Rosh Hashanah. Paul was so concerned about their devotion to the law that he voiced his worry that his work with the Galatians may have been wasted.

Theological Explanation

Through a series of arguments, Paul made it quite clear that he believed Christians are no longer subject to the law of Moses. Before Christ came, the law had an important function—one of preparing people for the Messiah. Because the messiah has come, we are no longer under the rule of the Old Testament law. *What specific guidelines must Christians follow, though?*

Of course, Paul said that Christians receive the Holy Spirit and are "clothed" with Christ, but these truths do not answer the myriad of questions that arise concerning moral and immoral behavior. David Koresh claimed to be inspired by the Spirit as his Branch Davidian cult stockpiled weapons. In Virginia, a mountain preacher took a second wife and claimed to be following the example of many Old Testament patriarchs. What did Paul have to say about this?

Part of Paul's answer is in Galatians 5:13-26. This question points out one reason why many of Paul's letters were collected and included in the canon of the New Testament. No one letter says all that needs to be said. Actually, Galatians, read by itself, gives far more stress to freedom from the law than it does to ethical imperatives, but this imbalance is nicely corrected by 1 Corinthians, where Paul corralled a congregation that had been living on the wild side. Perhaps the best solution is to read 1 Corinthians as soon as you finish Galatians.

What about *women*? If Paul really meant what he said in 3:28 about "no longer male and female," why did he insist that only women keep their heads covered when praying or speaking in worship (1 Cor 11:2-16)? How could he have told women to keep silent in church (1 Cor 14:33-36)?

First, the basic principle of equality through faith for Jew and Gentile, slave and free, male and female, lies at the heart of Paul's theology. In his day he was seen as a radical, and surely the radical way Jesus treated women as equals influenced Paul's viewpoint.

Second, for Paul, the equality of women was subsidiary to justification by faith and to spreading the news about that faith. Therefore, he wanted women to avoid offending the cultural standards of the day whenever possible. It was radical enough for them to be allowed to pray and preach ("prophesying" in 1 Cor 11:5) in worship, but for them to create a scandal by removing the traditional veils in worship would be selfish. Also, the women who asked questions aloud in worship were simply disruptive. Paul did not want scandal to hinder his message of faith in Christ, but he did believe that the unity brought by faith was so great that the differences that divided men and women faded into insignificance. Both men and women could pray in worship and preach (or prophesy). They were one in Christ.

What can we say about Paul's use of masculine language for God? If he called God "*Abba*! Father!"—why did he not also use the Aramaic and Greek terms for "Mother"? Even if he did not, should we?

Consider the three traditional barriers between people that Paul declared to be essentially obliterated: Jew/Gentile, slave/free, male/female. In none of the cases did he allow the obliteration of the human distinctions to change his language for God. Gentiles may have been justified the same way as Jews were, but God was still the God of Abraham, Isaac, and Jacob. Gentiles would not be made to feel "more equal" by occasionally using Gentile names for God like "Zeus" or "Apollo." Likewise, with Christ, slaves became equal to their owners spiritually, but they were expected to continue to call God by the traditional terms, "Lord" and "Master." The same held true for women of Paul's day. They were indeed equal to men in God's sight, but the biblical term "Father" was to be used. Women would not be made "more equal" by calling God "Mother."

Questions for Discussion

1. Do you agree with Paul that the law's purpose has ended? Is the Mosaic law of any positive value today?

2. Do you remember thinking of Christianity as essentially a set of rules and regulations? Is following Christ easier or more difficult?

3. How does your church apply Galatians 3:28 today? What leadership roles are open to women? How are other biblical passages dealt with that imply a subordinate status for women?

4. What terms for God are considered acceptable in your church? Is God still called "Father"? Does anyone use the term "Mother"? When discussing our language for God, be sure to distinguish between the use of simile and metaphor.

Note

[1]Richard N. Longenecker, *Galatians*, Word Biblical Commentary (Dallas: Word Books, 1990) 141-43.

Chapter 6

Set Free by Christ

Galatians 4:8–5:12

Though Paul's style of writing changed to a friendlier and more personal tone in this section, he still argued against enslavement to the law and in favor of freedom in Christ. He took care to direct his anger at the Judaizers rather than at the Galatians themselves. This section of the letter is composed of three parts: appeal to friendship (4:12-20), allegory of Sarah and Hagar (4:21-31), and freedom in Christ versus slavery under the law (5:1-12).

Paul's personal comments in the first section, an addendum to the autobiographical sketch of 1:11-2:14, allow us to learn a bit more about his first trip to Galatia and the formation of the church there. The second section raises difficult questions about the interpretation of scripture. Allegorical interpretation is particularly frowned upon by critical scholars today, but Paul used that method to apply the Sarah and Hagar story to his own situation. The toughest question needs to be asked: Is this a legitimate way to understand this story? Finally, the third section is easier to understand but raises a controversial question about apostasy and perseverance.

Comment

12 The warmer, more personal tone of this section is signaled by the affectionate address, "Friends" (literally, "Brothers"), as well as by the words, "I beg you." Paul wanted the Galatians to emulate his behavior. He reminded them that he had adopted their law-free lifestyle already.

13-14 Apparently Paul had not originally planned to visit in Galatia and establish churches, but a physical illness made him stop and seek help. The Galatians could easily have refused to help him, or they could have helped him but concluded that any missionary who was ill was not protected by a very powerful god. Instead, they took Paul in and received his message gladly. Many of them responded by professing faith in Jesus as the Christ. For these reasons, Paul loved the Galatians deeply.

15 Paul appealed to their mutual affection. He still cared for them, but had the Galatians lost their good feelings for him? His comment that they would have gladly given Paul their eyes may suggest that the physical ailment mentioned in verses 13-14 included an eye problem. Further evidence for this possibility might be the large letters that Paul used when he wrote the last few verses of the letter with his own hand (see 6:11). If his vision never fully recovered he would have had to write with large letters. Possibly, the reference to tearing out their eyes was an idiomatic expression that referred to a general willingness of the Galatians to help. In that case, we are left guessing as to the nature of Paul's illness.

16 In the first century, as in the twentieth, many people did not want to hear the truth if it was unpleasant. Not many preachers today, this one included, have the courage to tell their congregations the truth as bluntly as did Paul. An exception was Clarence Jordan, who boldly established an interracial farm in southern Georgia during the 1940s. After hearing him preach concerning the need for interracial fellowship, one elderly woman verbally attacked him:

> "I want you to know that my grandfather fought in the Civil War, and I'll never believe a word you say." Jordan replied, "Ma'am, your choice seems quite clear. It is whether you will follow your granddaddy or Jesus Christ."[1]

Paul's deep affection for the Galatian Christians did not prevent him from telling them unpleasant truths.

17-18 Another unpleasant truth was that the Judaizers were "courting" the Galatians with impure motives. The attention they paid to the Galatians was only for the purpose of excluding them, both from Paul and from the assurance of their prior justification. Cut off from Paul and doubting the sufficiency of their faith to provide justification, they would be at the mercy of the Judaizers. Then the Galatians would have to "court" the Judaizers to request education and guidance regarding the Jewish law. Paul hoped his readers would examine for purity the motives of anyone who seemed to court their favor.

19-20 Perhaps realizing that his anger at the Judaizers was detracting from the point he really wanted to make in this section of the letter, Paul resumed the warm, personal, tone he had evidenced in 4:12-15. He affectionately called the Galatians his "little children," and compared the pain he felt for their distress to the pain every mother feels during the birth of her children. Today such language would seem condescending to church members, but remember that all the Galatians were "baby Christians," and that most—if not all—of them had been converted by the testimony and preaching of Paul. He had a right to feel like their mother!

21 Paul began his final argument against pursuing justification through obedience to the Law. He asked if those who wanted so badly to be subject to the law of Moses knew the content of the law—that is, the first five books of the Old Testament.

22 Paul introduced the story of Abraham and the sons he bore by two different women—one by his wife Sarah and the other by his wife's slave, Hagar. The story deals with God's fulfillment of his second promise to Abraham that he would have a son and become the father of a great nation. Paul assumed that his readers knew the basic story; perhaps he had repeated the story to the Galatians when he preached and taught in Galatia. His interpretation is difficult to follow unless one is familiar with the basic story (see Gen 16:1-16; 21:1-14).

23 Paul's opponents had probably used this story as proof that they, Abraham's descendants through his son Isaac, were favored by God. The Galatians were fortunate to have the opportunity to join this "great nation" by agreeing to obey the Jewish law, or at least certain key statutes of that law. Paul set out to show that this biblical story did not support his opponents' position. Correctly interpreted, he believed, the story helped prove his point.

Rather than call Sarah and Hagar by their names, Paul referred to them as "the slave" and "the free woman." By using this nomenclature he could set up the free/slave distinction at the beginning of his interpretation. Of course,

Genesis makes it clear that both boys were conceived in the normal way, "according to the flesh," but Sarah's son Isaac was the only one through whom God would fulfill the promise to Abraham (see Gen 17:15-21).

24 Rather than translate the Greek verb, *allegoreo*, to mean "this is an allegory" (as does the NRSV), it is preferable to take it to mean that this story can be "interpreted allegorically." In other words, Paul was not insisting that the story was originally written as an allegory, but only that it could be interpreted with the allegorical method.

Paul's use of allegorical interpretation causes many modern scholars to wince. Today this method of interpreting scripture is widely disparaged because it has often been used to make the Bible say anything the interpreter desires. Medieval interpreters used the allegorical method to devalue the original historical events in scripture and substitute their own more "spiritual" interpretations. Having noted the dangers of the allegorical method, I must add that Paul's interpretation does not deny the importance of the historical Sarah and Hagar as the more extreme forms of allegorical interpretation might. Paul had previously stressed the importance of the historical Abraham and simply sought to find an additional meaning beneath the historical text. Modern scholars often refer to this rather mild form of allegory as "typology."

25-26 Paul's identification of Hagar with Mount Sinai in Arabia is at first puzzling, for Hagar had nothing to do with the giving of the Ten Commandments at Mount Sinai. In fact, many ancient scribes who were making copies of Galatians thought they needed to correct the verse. As you can see from the footnote in the NRSV, they "corrected" the verse to read, "For Sinai is a mountain in Arabia." Paul identified Hagar with Mount Sinai because her descendants through Ishmael, the Arabs, lived south of Israel in the region near Mount Sinai. Now comes Paul's key interpretive move. He associated Mount Sinai, where the law was delivered to Moses, with the present-day Jerusalem, the center of law-based Judaism. By establishing the links between the slave woman (Hagar), Mount Sinai, and the present Jerusalem, Paul could conclude that Jerusalem "is in slavery with her children." Of course, those enslaved children were Paul's opponents, the Judaizers.

The second half of the puzzle concerning Hagar and Mount Sinai is easy to solve. The free woman, Sarah, was associated with "the Jerusalem above" and all those who were children through faith—like Paul. They were "free," meaning free from bondage to the law. Referring to the "Jerusalem above" was a common way for Jews and Christians to symbolize their hope for God's transformation of the world or creation of a new world. Revelation 21:2 describes a "new Jerusalem" coming down from heaven.

27 The quotation from Isaiah 54:1 was chosen because of its reference to the "childless one." In Isaiah the passage refers to the time of Israel's exile in Babylonia, nearly a thousand years after the lifetime of Abraham and Sarah. According to Paul's interpretation, however, the promise that the "childless" woman would eventually have more children than the woman "who has a husband" (NIV) applied to Sarah and Hagar. Hagar had a husband (meaning she had a child by Abraham), while Sarah was still barren, though eventually Sarah would have more children. Paul meant that Sarah was the mother of all who believed in Christ, both Jews and Gentiles.

28 This is the theological payoff to Paul's interpretation. The Galatians themselves were children of Sarah, just as Isaac was, and like Isaac, they were children of the promise that God made to Abraham—as long as they trusted in Christ, just as Abraham trusted in God's promise.

29 According to Jewish oral tradition, Ishmael picked on his little half-brother Isaac, but there is no biblical evidence of Ishmael's persecution of Isaac. We have evidence that Jews persecuted Christians in Paul's day (see Acts 13:50-51; 1 Thess 2:14-16). Possibly the Judaizers hoped to prevent persecution by non-Christian Jews by convincing the Gentile Christians to honor the law of Moses.

30-31 Paul concluded by quoting Genesis 21:10 and applying the verse to the situation in Galatia. Just as Sarah told Abraham to drive out the slave woman and her child, so the Galatians should drive away the Judaizers who were associated with slavery to the law. In regard to the law, the Galatians must see that they were "free."

The entire allegorical interpretation raises many difficult issues that are beyond the scope of this volume. (For an excellent treatment, see Longenecker, 198-217.)

5:1 Verse 1 serves both as a conclusion to the Sarah and Hagar story and as an introduction to Paul's passionate plea to choose liberty over slavery in 5:2-12. It is strikingly similar to Jesus' discussion of freedom and slavery found in John 8:31-36. In both instances the listeners were tempted to rely on Jewish heritage (law) and found it difficult to believe that they could be slaves in any sense. Jesus tried to convince his listeners that he could set them free, and Paul reminded the Galatians that they had already been set free by Christ.

2 The practical question facing the Galatians was whether the males among them would allow themselves to be circumcised by the Judaizers. This would symbolize their willingness to accept the Jewish law as a supplement to faith in Christ. Apparently they had not yet done this but were seriously considering the possibility. Paul himself was circumcised as a baby, and Acts 16:1-3 tells us that he circumcised Timothy, whose mother was Jewish. Presumably Paul would have had no objections to the modern American practice of circumcising infants for medical reasons, but he certainly did object to circumcising Gentiles for religious reasons! In effect, he said that if you do not trust Christ enough to rely on him without the additional benefit of circumcision, then your "faith" is not strong enough to be of any benefit to you.

3 Furthermore, the Galatians should not think that the ritual of circumcision and obedience to a few food laws would suffice. If they wished to submit to the law of Moses, they must obey every ordinance of that law.

4 What exactly did Paul mean by saying that any Galatians who sought justification through the law had thereby "fallen away from grace"? Did he mean that they had lost their salvation? This passage has long troubled Baptists, who generally hold to Calvin's view that true salvation can never be lost. Paul did not actually say that any of the Galatians had lost their salvation, but he did seem to warn against "apostasy" as a real danger.

5 In contrast, the Galatians who relied on faith alone could await God's judgment without fear. God had sent the Holy Spirit to them as a guarantee of their justification (see Gal 3:2-5). Their righteousness would become that of Jesus Christ himself.

6 Paul clearly stated that the physical act of circumcision was neither negative nor positive. We forget what a radical statement this was for a first-century Jew to make! He was not really concerned with the act of circumcision itself; the attitude of the Galatians concerned him—their lack of certainty that faith alone would be sufficient.

When Martin Luther translated a similar passage in Romans, he insisted on the translation, "justified by faith *alone*." Many Baptists have agreed with Luther's phrase for the wrong reasons. They have taught that salvation is automatically granted when one walks the aisle and makes a public profession of faith, even if that faith is not accompanied by any subsequent change in the person's life or lifestyle. Clearly Paul did *not* conceive of faith in that way. Faith does include what we call "beliefs," but it is more than that. True faith, for Paul, is "faith working through love." The results will be visible.

7-8 Before their recent crisis, the Galatians had been growing spiritually. Paul reiterated that the Judaizers, whom he never called by name, were persuading the Galatians to move away from the one who called them to faith—away from God.

9 Paul cited what must have been a well-known proverb, applying it, naturally, to the Judaizers. Only a little of their teaching could affect the whole church.

10 Throughout Galatians Paul's confidence level seemed to oscillate. In verses 2-4 he sounded like the battle was almost lost, but in verse 10 he was more confident. He wanted to make sure that the Galatians realized that his anger was not directed at them but at the Judaizers—they would pay the penalty!

11 Verse 11 seems to make no sense. Who would accuse Paul of preaching circumcision? Certainly no one who reads this letter! Apparently some of his opponents had said something to the effect that Paul taught circumcision elsewhere, but when he arrived in Galatia he watered down the requirements for salvation by dispensing with circumcision. Perhaps they had heard that Paul had circumcised someone like Timothy (Acts 16:1-3). Obviously they had misread the man from Tarsus.

12 At the beginning of the letter (1:8-9), Paul had called a curse upon his opponents because of the dangerous way they were perverting the gospel and later expressed a wish that those knife-happy Judaizers would "castrate themselves" (accurately translated in the NRSV)! His language was crude, but perhaps it awakened the Galatians to the danger they were facing.

Theological Reflection

The sharpness of Paul's language raised an important issue that crystallized in his question: "Have I now become your enemy by telling you the truth?" How should we deal with conflicting viewpoints in our churches? Some Baptist churches are torn by strife at least partly because various members attack one another. Our entire denomination has split into several warring camps, and many harsh words have been written and spoken about fellow Christians. At the same time, many churches keep differing viewpoints hidden, do not air differences, and insure that virtually all the votes in business meetings are unanimous.

What can we learn from Galatians about speaking the truth? Perhaps Paul has taught us that the central truth of the gospel *must* be worth fighting for. His words were harsh, but his version of Christianity really was incompatible with the version promoted by the Judaizers. This bold defense of the truth of the gospel must be combined with the wisdom to differentiate between crucial and peripheral issues. Furthermore, the bold statement of the truth ought only to come from Christians who care about one another as deeply as Paul did for the Galatians.

Paul's *interpretation* of the Old Testament is generally bold and illuminating. His use of the allegorical method of interpretation, however, raises many red flags today. To be brief—the method is dangerous. It allows the interpreter almost unlimited freedom to import meaning into a text that is totally unrelated to the text. In fairness to Paul, it must be said that even while allegorizing he never lost sight of the original story. God's promise to Abraham was fulfilled only through the child he bore with Sarah, and faith was essential to the fulfillment of the promise.

For those who still try to memorize scripture, one of the finest verses to learn is 5:6b: "The only thing that counts is *faith working through love.*" Since so much of Galatians absolutely blasts those who want to add works of the law to faith, Paul's words can be easily misunderstood. He did not mean that all constraints against immoral behavior can be dropped. A Christian cannot cheat on his wife, steal from her company, spend money selfishly, skip worship, tell racist jokes, ignore the poor, and then expect to be justified "by faith alone." No! Paul defined faith as "faith working through love." The true Christian will be filled with love for God and love for his or her neighbors. If that love is not guided by the law of Moses, what specific guidelines did Paul give to show Christians how love acts? For that answer, read the next chapter.

Questions for Discussion

1. What truths would get your pastor in trouble (or even fired) if he/she voiced them openly in your congregation? What is the most painful truth your congregation has received from a minister who loved you?

2. What do you think about Paul's interpretation of the Sarah and Hagar story? What do you see as the benefits of this non-literal reading of the story? What are the dangers of this method of interpretation?

3. If you have already professed faith in Christ, what changes has God caused in your life because of that faith?

4. Southern Baptist churches have several million "non-resident members." Some of these people maintain that membership for sentimental reasons, but others give every indication of having abandoned their faith. Do you think that possibly some of them have "fallen away from grace?"

5. Give an example of someone in your church who best demonstrates "faith working through love."

Note

[1]C. Douglas Weaver, *A Cloud of Witnesses: Sermon Illustrations and Devotionals from the Christian Heritage* (Macon GA: Smyth & Helwys, 1993) 155.

Chapter 7

Freedom Guided by Love

Galatians 5:13–6:18

It is amazing that the Christians in Galatia considered circumcision at all. Circumcision was widely ridiculed throughout the Roman Empire. Even pagans who greatly admired Judaism's high ethical standards made fun of this "barbaric" ritual that the Jews imposed upon baby boys and adult male converts. The requirement of circumcision severely limited the number of adult male converts to Judaism in the ancient world. How many grown men today would consent to this operation?

The Galatians must have feared some great danger even more than the surgeon's knife. What danger could have driven them to consider the Judaizer's offer of circumcision? That danger must have been the reappearance of immoral behavior among the members of their churches. Even though they had experienced the Spirit and had faith in Christ—sometimes a faith that worked through love— they lived in a very immoral society and were daily tempted to revert to their former pagan lifestyles. As certain members began to fall back into their old habits and commit sins openly, the Galatians faced a crisis. They needed some specific ethical guidelines; they needed someone to set behavioral parameters beyond which they would not venture. Making a commitment to obey the law of Moses seemed to be a practical way to receive some very specific ethical guidelines. They needed this ethical guidance so badly that they were even willing to consider the trauma of adult circumcision at the hands of the Judaizers. What could Paul offer as an alternative?

Comment

13 Paul was at least aware of the problem facing the Galatians. Some of them were excusing their self-indulgent, sinful behavior under the guise of "freedom." Instead, true freedom is freedom from the obsession with the "flesh" that one's own sinful nature encourages. The Christian is not free from obligation to others or to God.

14 Verse 14 is the key to Paul's understanding of the Mosaic law and Christian moral behavior. After all his negative comments about the law, it is surprising that he said something positive about the law being "fulfilled" ("summed up" in NRSV). Stephen Westerholm has shown that Paul was not inconsistent at this point. Instead, Paul very carefully used two different Greek verbs, meaning "do" and "fulfill," regarding the law. He never said Christians are to "do" the law's commands; he said Christian behavior "fulfills" the law.[1]

Paul's language about fulfilling the law is consistent with Jesus' words concerning the law in Matthew 5:17: "I have come not to abolish but to fulfill." Note that Paul chose to quote Leviticus 19:18, the same verse Jesus used as the basis for his parable of the good Samaritan (Luke 10:25-37). According to both Jesus and Paul, God's real purpose for the law was fulfilled as Christians demonstrated love for their neighbors.

15 Obviously, some of the Galatians had not exactly treated each other with loving kindness. They had attacked each other like wild animals. Such behavior convinced them they needed stricter moral guidelines.

16-17 The NRSV translates verse 16 as a double exhortation: "Live by the Spirit . . . and do not gratify the desires of the flesh." The verse is better translated as a promise, however, as in the NIV: "Live by the flesh, *and you will not* gratify the desires of the flesh" (emphasis added). Those Christians who turn control of their lives over to the Holy Spirit will find the Spirit moving them in a different direction than their flesh or sinful nature would prefer. Turning one's life over to the Spirit is not easy to do, for Christians experience an internal war between the Spirit and the flesh (or sinful nature) that often prevents them from doing what they originally intended. (Paul later elaborated upon this internal struggle in Romans 7:7-25.)

18 Two solutions to the problem of temptation by one's own sinful nature are: following the law or following the Spirit. The Galatians who took Paul's advice and allowed the Spirit to lead their lives were not subject to the law of Moses. Westerholm thinks that Paul "may have been the first to see the indwelling spirit as the abiding guide and enabler of Christian moral behavior."[2]

19-21 Many scholars devalue this list of sins because it was similar to other lists of vices published in the ancient world. Therefore, it was not distinctively "Pauline." This list probably gives us a good idea of some of the specific sins that were disrupting the sense of fellowship among the Galatians. Furthermore, it reminds us that Paul did not endorse "situation ethics"—none of the actions he listed show love for others; none of these sins are inspired by the Spirit.

The fifteen sins listed can be grouped into four categories: sexual sins, religious deviations, interpersonal abuse, and sins involving substance abuse.[3] A few of these terms may be unclear to modern readers: "Fornication" refers to sexual relations outside marriage, specifically to pre-marital sex. "Sorcery" is a synonym for witchcraft. (One wonders what Paul would say about the decision of one of the country's leading divinity schools—not a Baptist one—to invite a self-proclaimed witch to speak in chapel.) "Enmities" would be better translated "hatred" or "quarrels."

Paul considered these sins to be so serious that he repeated a warning he had previously given to the Galatians in person: "Those who do such things will not inherit the kingdom of God." He did not mean that one's salvation could be lost by a single sinful act. His use of a present participle meant that he was referring to repeated, regular sinful behavior. Some of the Galatians were in danger of relapsing into a full-blown pagan lifestyle, and Paul was definitely warning them that people who lived like that would not be saved! He described salvation as an inheritance of "the kingdom of God," using Jesus' favorite phrase instead of his more typical terminology—"justification" or "in Christ."

22-23 The Spirit does not merely prohibit evil behavior; it engenders Christlike behavior. Paul listed nine "fruits of the Spirit" to remind the Galatians of the type of behavior that should be characteristic of their church. Quite intentionally, Paul listed first the *agape* love that he described so well in 1 Corinthians 13. For him, this was the chief characteristic of a Christian lifestyle, with all the other virtues arising from a deep love for God and for others. This love could not be commanded by the Mosaic law, but could be created within by the work of the Spirit.

24 The reference to "crucifying the flesh" gave a backward glance at the cross, reminding the Galatian readers that their opportunity for a new moral life was not cost free. It also shows how totally opposed Christian ethics must be to the contemporary "talk-show ethics." Seemingly in Hollywood, the way to justify a particular lifestyle or behavior is to demonstrate how widespread and "natural" the underlying desire is that leads to such behavior. Paul granted that such desires and passions occur naturally, but he insisted that they be "crucified."

25-26 Among scholars, Paul was famous for his "indicative/imperative." That means he first described our experience of salvation with an indicative—"we live by the Spirit"—and followed that with the imperative—"let us also be guided by the Spirit."[4] Paul seemingly added three more items that might more properly be included in the list of sins found in verses 19-21. The next ten verses elaborate upon these three particular sins, so Paul had good reason to mention them separately from the earlier list.

6:1 After reading verse 6:1 and recalling Paul's harsh remarks about curses and castration, one of my church members asked a tough question: "Did Paul heed his own advice?" The only possible answer is that Paul considered heresy more serious than typical moral transgressions. Thus, he would have defended his harsh attack on the Judaizers on the basis of the grave danger they presented to the true gospel. He felt that a verbal blitzkrieg was necessary to prevent the Galatians from falling from grace.

How do we apply Paul's words in the church today? How do we typically deal with Christians who have committed an obvious sin? Most churches either choose to ignore the sin and act as if nothing has happened, or else they react harshly and make the person no longer feel welcome in the congregation. A gentle correction, however, reminds people that Christians are held accountable for their behavior while still conveying the love that was at the heart of Paul's message.

2-5 In verses 2-5, we face another exhortation that at first glance seems self-contradictory. Did Paul want us to "bear one another's burdens" (v. 2) or allow all people to "carry their own loads" (v. 5)? First, note that two different terms are used. Verse 2 continues Paul's advice about correcting another Christian who had sinned. Those sins are the "burdens" of the other person we are asked to bear. We are asked to help bring them back into right relationship with God and with the church, though this could easily lead to spiritual pride as the "helper" compares himself or herself with the "helpee." The helper's attitude could easily become like that of the Pharisee whose attitude Jesus mimicked in Luke 18:11: "God, I thank you that I am not like other people—thieves, rogues, adulterers, or even like this tax collector." This Pharisee was not fit to restore anyone else from sin; neither is anyone else whose attitude resembles that of the Pharisee.

Paul did not want Christians comparing themselves to others. While helping to restore others, Christians must evaluate their own behavior ("test their own work"). That daily behavior is the "load" (v. 5) that Christians must carry for themselves. Hopefully, they can carry their own loads on a daily basis and also have enough love for others to "fulfill the law of Christ." That law was quoted earlier: "Love your neighbor as yourself" (5:14).

6 Verse 6 is the favorite verse of most pastor/teachers. In addition to evaluating their own behavior and occasionally helping to restore a brother or sister who had sinned,

Paul also wanted the Galatians to provide material support (food, clothing, and/or money) for the church's teachers.

7-8 Paul gave a decisive rebuttal to anyone who thought that "justification by faith alone" meant saving faith could ever exist without good works. True faith will lead a Christian to "sow to the Spirit"—that is, to demonstrate love for others. People who say they have "faith" but continually "sow to [their] own flesh" are mocking God and will reap "destruction" (NIV).

9-10 Although his language may have implied that some had already "mocked God" or "fallen away from grace," in actuality Paul never seemed to give up on any of his converts, but instead he encouraged them to persevere "in doing what is right." He always exhorted them to return to the Spirit-led life.

11 Paul often used a scribe to do the actual writing of his letters and then penned the final few sentences himself (see 1 Cor 16:21 or 2 Thess 3:17). Why did he write with "large letters," though? Perhaps Paul had a continuing eye problem, or he simply wished to give greater emphasis to his words, just as a larger font size was chosen for the chapter titles within this book. These are the two most plausible reasons for the large letters.

12 Using his own pen, Paul began to reiterate some of the points he made earlier about the Judaizers. For one thing, the Judaizers had hidden motives for encouraging the Galatians to accept circumcision. They wanted to gain status and, more to the point, avoid persecution by circumcising the Gentile Christians in Galatia. Remember that Christianity and Judaism had not yet separated into two distinct religions. Apparently, some of the most militant non-Christian Jews were threatening to persecute Jewish Christians because they heard of churches where Jews and uncircumcised Gentiles were intermingling. If the Galatians could all be persuaded to be circumcised, the Judaizers could defend themselves by saying that the Galatian church had no more Gentiles in it. Christianity would then be seen as a particular sect of Judaism. From Paul's perspective, such action was cowardice—a dropping of the cross of Christ in the face of persecution.

13-14 Paul added another complaint. The Judaizers themselves did not obey the law—that is, not the *whole* law. They practiced circumcision and perhaps kept the Sabbath and avoided pork, but they did not keep the whole law—not like Paul kept it before his conversion. Therefore, Paul, the ex-legalist, concluded that they were not really sincere. They desired to boast about the Galatians' flesh, but for Christians, the only appropriate boast would be of the cross.

The problem of inappropriate boasting was faced squarely by Charles Spurgeon after he finished preaching and an admirer gushed:

> Oh, Mr. Spurgeon, that was wonderful! Spurgeon responded, "Yes, madam—so the devil whispered into my ear as I came down the steps of the pulpit."[5]

Most ministers, myself included, have a difficult time remembering this lesson. Perhaps both ministers and laypeople need to stay more "cross-focused."

15-16 Paul nearly repeated an earlier comment about the relative unimportance of circumcision (or uncircumcision). That earlier verse showed that he believed God's "new creation" consisted of "faith working through love" in the life of a Spirit-led believer. His blessing of peace and mercy was given to all the Galatians who followed his teaching. Lacking circumcision, but having faith in Christ, these Gentile Christians were "the Israel of God." They were already children of Abraham, children of the promise.

17 Paul left us with one last enigma. What were the "marks of Jesus," and how did Paul acquire them? Paul probably referred to scars that he bore as a result of persecution for the gospel. He was nearly stoned to death in the Galatian city of Lystra (Acts 14:19). Five times he received thirty-nine lashes at the hands of the Jews (2 Cor 11:24). Surely such severe punishment left scars, which the apostle considered his "marks of Jesus." Because their version of the gospel was not as offensive to non-Christian Jews, the Judaizers suffered no such persecution. From Paul's perspective, they had no right to continue to trouble him.

18 As hot as Paul's anger burned, his love for the Galatians still allowed him to conclude by sending God's grace (not law!) upon the believers. They remained his brothers and sisters in Christ.

Theological Reflection

Paul's entire argument is misunderstood if he is seen as simply opposing the law of Moses. Rather, he was trying to work out a solution to the great paradox in his life. Before his Damascus road experience, Paul lived for the law of Moses. He followed every statute to the letter. He was sure God had given the law, and he wanted to do exactly what God wanted. He discovered that this intense following of every detail of the law had led him to do the unthinkable—persecute God's messiah. Obviously Paul had misunderstood God's will. His attitude toward the law had to be radically reconsidered. In Galatians we see how he worked out a new solution. Echoing the words of Christ, Paul drove to the conclusion that the law is not to be "done" but to be "fulfilled." The whole law is fulfilled in the command, "Love your neighbor as yourself."

As profound as this approach to the law is, it lacks the specificity of his former legalistic approach in which every sin was defined. Without specific guidelines, the Galatians could easily have slipped back into an immoral pagan lifestyle and continued to think they were led by the Spirit. Paul attempted to solve this problem by listing numerous "works of the flesh" and balancing them with the desired behaviors or "fruits of the Spirit." He worked out this aspect of his theology much more thoroughly in the book of 1 Corinthians.

Paul's general guidelines for handling obvious sins committed by members of the congregation sounds outdated. We are not comfortable with interpersonal disagreement, so we find it easier to either ignore obvious sins or to make the "sinner" feel ostracized, so they leave the church permanently. Some churches favor one method over the other. Few churches seem able to do what is done in large companies all the time: a wrong is committed, the appropriate rebuke is given, feelings are hurt for a while but the behavior is changed, the person is told that he or she is still part of the team, and soon everybody is back to work. Could churches today possibly learn something about "conflict management" from Paul?

Finally, how successful was Paul's letter? Did most of the Galatians side with Paul, or did many of them choose circumcision at the hands of the Judaizers? Honestly, we do not know the answer. All we can say for certain is that Paul's letter was deeply respected by some of the Galatians. They appreciated his words enough to keep the letter for a decade or more until some unknown disciple of Paul's made a copy of it and included Galatians in a collection of Paul's letters.

In the long run, Paul's view triumphed and thousands of Gentiles began flooding into the early Christian church. Here was a new religion that offered a savior, a fellowship open to all, and high ethical standards. Many pagans who had admired Judaism found that Christianity offered what they liked about Judaism without requiring circumcision and food laws, which they considered barbaric and irrelevant, respectively. Paul's solution to the problem of the law gave Christianity a cross-cultural appeal that enabled it to spread around the world. Not many of us would be Christians today had he lost the argument.

Questions for Discussion

1. If the Gallup organization surveyed all the people who lived on your block, what percentage of them would say that they are sure you love them? Why?

2. Which sins of the list in 5:19-21 are still occasionally a problem for you?

3. Which "fruits of the Spirit" are most evident in your congregation? Name one church member who seems to specialize in each of the nine fruits.

4. Is there any sin that a person might commit that would cause him/her to receive even a mild rebuke from the congregation or pastor? Name the sin.

5. How might your perspective on Christianity be different if you had been stoned or whipped severely for your faith?

Notes

[1]Steven Westerholm, *Israel's Law and the Church's Faith* (Grand Rapids MI: Eerdmans, 1988) 204.

[2]Ibid., 213.

[3]See the helpful chart listing the sins and the translations chosen for them in six different versions of the Bible in: Ronald Y. K. Fung, *The Epistle to the Galatians*, New International Commentary on the New Testament (Grand Rapids MI: Eerdmans, 1988) 254.

[4]The verb translated "let us also be guided" is actually a hortatory subjunctive, but it is used as an imperative.

[5]C. Douglas Weaver, *A Cloud of Witnesses: Sermon Illustrations and Devotionals from the Christian Heritage* (Macon GA: Smyth & Helwys, 1993) 138-39.